GOD HAS
A COMMUNICATION
PROBLEM

GOD HAS
A COMMUNICATION
PROBLEM

Chester Pennington

HAWTHORN BOOKS, INC.
W. Clement Stone, Publisher
New York

GOD HAS A COMMUNICATION PROBLEM

Library of Congress Catalog Card Number: 75–28692

ISBN: 0–8015–3044–X

1 2 3 4 5 6 7 8 9 10

To Marjorie
who shares
the demands and delights
of our ministry

Contents

Contents

   viii

Introduction: An Invitation

God has a communication problem.
There is evidence that we are it.
You are invited to inquire
whether this may in fact be so,
and whether we may become
co-workers in relieving the problem.

This invitation is extended somewhat awkwardly but with a sense of urgency. Part of the awkwardness is that there are several things to be said at once, and it is difficult to know where to begin. Let me quickly try to state a concern, to issue the invitation, and to identify the inquiry.

The Concern

Almost everybody in the churches today—lay and clergy alike—agree that preaching is in trouble and indeed has been for some time. There seems to be evidence of increasing concern about the situation, which is encouraging. But let us look at the circumstances as they are at this present moment.

Laypeople say, "I wish I could hear better sermons. I'm hungry for good preaching." Sometimes they are more direct and ask bluntly, "Why can't preachers preach? They just don't say anything that impresses me as interesting or important." I am not sure how often clergy hear these remarks. That is one reason for this invitation: to let clergy hear laity.

On the other hand, ministers often say, "We're not sure sermons are all that important. There must be better ways of communication. Besides we have too many other things to do." Frankly, I doubt that preachers often talk like this to members of their churches. That is another reason for the invitation: to let laity hear clergy.

The Invitation

This, then, is an invitation to laity and clergy to look into the whole subject of preaching. Is it important? Does it need or deserve improvement, or should it be abandoned in favor of other means of communication? The invitation is issued with a sense that now is an opportune time to engage in such an inquiry.

• One of the most encouraging signs in our churches today is a recovery of interest in preaching—on the part of preachers themselves. It may seem ironic to put it that way, but it is an accurate reflection of the circumstances.

Thoughtful laypersons have been concerned about preaching quite consistently and for a long time. It is preachers and their teachers who have had the most serious doubts about whether preaching really matters. Today there is evidence —welcome to many of us—that among clergy, teachers of clergy, and students preparing for the ministry, there is a renewed recognition that what happens on Sundays in the worshiping congregation is important, and that, in such a context, preaching has a special significance.

So the invitation is extended to clergy to consider the subject of preaching in general and your own preaching in particular. How important is it? How effective is it? Are you satisfied with the quality of your preaching? Is it worth the trouble of working at it?

• Hearing sermons is just as important as preaching them. And hearing includes, not just listening on Sundays, but responding all week long with agreement or disagreement or requests for clarification, with honest efforts to implement a common faith, with support of the church and its ministries.

So the invitation is extended to laypersons. If you really think preaching is important—or can be—you may find this inquiry helpful. You are invited to look at preaching from the inside. What would you like to have happen in a sermon? What has to be done in order for it to happen? Your own informed understanding of preaching will contribute to the quality of the final result.

• Basically, this is God's problem too. If what we believe about the church is true, God is concerned about how effectively the gospel is preached and celebrated by ministers and congregations. Apparently, he has difficulty getting this done well.

A sensitive reading of Scripture certainly indicates that God has a communication problem. The scriptural account of his dealings with us suggests that he has "one earth of a time" communicating his message, even to his chosen people.

Again and again he says to them (us), "This is what I want you to do."

Just as often they (we) reply, "We know well enough what you want us to do, but we'd like to try our own way."

He warns, "You're liable to destroy yourselves."

And they (we) respond, "We'll take our chances."

And they did (we do) with recorded results—usually disastrous (just read history or the newspapers).

Among the heroes of Scripture are the Hebrew prophets, such as Amos, Hosea, Isaiah, Jeremiah. They were the great preachers of their day, and we revere them as fearless proclaimers of God's word to his people.

The simple fact is that in their own day the prophets did not win. We rightly honor them as courageous men whose insights have been vindicated by history, but their own contemporaries were not persuaded by these preachers. Leaders and people alike refused to follow the message of the prophets. And for all the reverence we give them (safely removed by twenty-five hundred years), there is plenty of evidence that most of us do not really take their message seriously either.

Even God's supreme effort at communication in Jesus Christ carried with it, and still carries with it, no guarantee that it would be either understood or accepted. The amazingly honest Gospels indicate that Jesus' closest associates often misunderstood him, and many others who seemed to understand rejected him. Any equally honest account of our world and our churches must admit that the misunderstanding and the rejection still go on.

The invitation, then, is to engage in an inquiry that we dare to believe is important to God as well as to us. He wants to communicate his will and his grace. He may indeed have many ways of doing this, but there is evidence that he has trouble getting through to us. We are reluctant to listen when addressed by God, and we are not always able to pass the message along. But he keeps trying. Some of us believe that preaching is one of the instruments God would like to use, even though it suffers from many limitations and hindrances.

We venture to hope that in our inquiry God will communicate with us. If we listen and learn, he may be able also to communicate through us.

The Inquiry

In a way, this is a personal document. I write after thirty years of work in the parish ministry plus three years of teaching in a school of theology. The past three years have given me a chance to reflect on what I had been doing for three decades. They have also afforded me the opportunity to do research in areas which have direct relevance to the tasks of preaching and hearing sermons. This inquiry, then, is intended to be marked by both personal reflection and intellectual seriousness. What has been learned in parish experience will be related to what is learned in academic disciplines, and vice versa. So if the manner is occasionally informal, the intent is serious.

Our inquiry will be limited to preaching. This means that there are many important subjects that we cannot deal with at all or only in passing. For instance, throughout all my ministry, my primary concern has been for theology: what we believe and why and what difference it makes. The basic issues confronting us in church and civilization are theological: What is the meaning of human existence? How may we find fulfillment? How does what we believe about God and Christ and ourselves relate to all this? For thirty years, I have wrestled with these questions in company with several congregations. They have been exciting years. Now, in this inquiry, we are not talking about the substance of preaching but about the act of delivering and listening to sermons. Obviously, serious theological discussion will have to be limited, even though I believe that is where the basic issues are.

Similarly, we all recognize that there are many facets to our experiences together in our churches. Corporate worship is only one aspect of church life, and preaching is only one means of communication. In this study, we will acknowledge the richness and variety of congregational life and try to relate preaching to the whole context. But we can consider carefully only one subject, the preaching and hearing of sermons.

Before completing the boundaries of our inquiry, let me add a few considerations which may help clarify my intentions.

• *Preacher* is not my favorite title for members of the ordained clergy. But it designates the specific function th t w are examining. Therefore, I shall use the term preacher more freely than usual, not so much as a title for clergy, as an indicator of the task being studied.

• This inquiry is intended, not simply for the specially gifted person or the large church with a multiple staff, but for all of us. My hope is to offer reflections and suggestions which will be useful for any preacher and any church member anywhere. Most ministers work as the only pastor serving the congregation, doing all the tasks that a single leader must do, plus many others that were never anticipated. These pages are written for them and even for the ministers who are not sure that preaching is their principal talent but who must exercise it week after week. Most local churches have only one pastor and a modest budget, but they want and deserve good preaching. These pages are written for them. I believe that the church on Main Street, Smalltown, U.S.A., deserves as effective preaching as First Church in Metropolis.

So the invitation to engage in this inquiry is extended to all preachers and all laypersons. If you happen to be a person with special talent or a member of a church with unusual resources, you are lucky. This discussion may be useful to all of us.

• My concern as a teacher of preaching is not to develop "great preachers," but to sharpen the skills of all preachers. What we need is, not more "great" preachers, but a greater number of more competent preachers. It is wise to define our expectations very carefully at this point.

Criticism of preaching is often expressed in a question: "If preaching is so important, why aren't there more great preachers?"

My answer is another question: "How many great people in any occupation are there?" How many great teachers? Doctors? Scientists? Politicians? There must be thousands of entertainers working in the United States, but how many stars are there? Greatness is a quality achieved by only a few persons of extraordinary gifts, and this is true in any field you mention. It is certainly true in preaching.

There are and always will be only a few great preachers. Most of us are persons of modest gifts. What is important is, not that we strive to be great, but that we aim to be as good as we can be. The imperative of excellence is laid on all of us. Every preacher can be a good craftsman, and my aim is to help preachers become persons who know their business and do it well.

In all honesty, I have to add that underlying such competence there must be an authentic commitment to the task—to the one whom we serve, to the faith we teach. This is basic to everything else, but it cannot be the primary concern of our present study. Our aim here is to enable each other to become persons who know how to communicate our deepest convictions, to share our faith, to speak winsomely about our Lord.

Let us as clergy take a fresh look at our preaching. We all have typical insecurities and misgivings; some of these are valid and should be dealt with, some are merely nuisances to be put up with. Let's sort them out. There are basic insights that we have known for years but may have neglected. Let's look at them again. I should like to encourage you to undertake the task of preaching with renewed interest and confidence and effectiveness.

Let us as laity look at preaching in ways that may be somewhat different from our usual perspective. I should like to invite you into the pastor's study to see the work that must go on there, because what happens there determines what happens on Sunday. Let me share some confidences that you may not have heard before. And let's look also at laity's part in preaching to learn what you can contribute to the making of sermons.

The conviction underlying this inquiry is that the more

clergy and laity understand about the process of communication, the more effectively we can engage in it. This will
surely result in the enrichment of our lives together, both in
church and in society. And if, in fact, God is trying to communicate with us, who knows what might happen.

PART 1

THE RENEWAL OF
PREACHING

1
A Place to Start

Every inquiry has to begin somewhere. This one starts with two basic presuppositions: (1) Preaching is the primary means of communication in the church; (2) If there is to be any significant improvement in the quality of preaching, both laity and clergy must help it happen. Let's look at these two assumptions.

Preaching as Central

Preaching is the primary means by which a minister communicates with the congregation. This probably seems self-evident to most laypersons, but it is not at all self-evident to many ministers. A good many clergy have serious doubts about the importance of preaching; so I want to stake out this presupposition rather carefully.

In the italicized sentence, note first that the adjective is *primary.* It is not claimed that preaching is the only means, but that it is the primary among several means of communication in the life of the congregation. Preaching will be accompanied by other occasions for communication: small groups of many kinds, varieties of study groups, administrative structures, personal relationships. But central to all these, giving shape and direction to the whole effort, is preaching.

This understanding can be supported by simple, practical observation. There are theological defenses of preaching, and with a personal love for theology, I respect these arguments. But they are singularly ineffective with skeptics and quite unnecessary for believers. I would rather offer a simple observation about the life of any typical congregation: *The Sunday service of worship is the principal, perhaps the only, occasion on which a minister has the opportunity to communicate with significant numbers of the congregation.* Once this fact is clearly seen, the central importance of preaching is evident.

According to national statistics, thirty-five to forty percent of all church members attend services on any given Sunday. The percentage is not made up of the same persons, but it remains impressively steady. Add to this number a sprinkling of nonmembers, who are there for a variety of reasons. In typical parishes, that is the only occasion on which pastors can communicate with that many of the people in the parish. Not all the congregational programs taken together, plus all of the personal pastoral contacts, will reach that large a segment of the congregation. It is a matter of simple arithmetic—or rather of profound arithmetic. We are not merely counting numbers; we are reaching persons.

People come to church with their needs and concerns, and the sermon may be the minister's only opportunity to address these personal problems. In a congregation of any size, the pastor may not see some of the church members until next Sunday, when they will be there again. It is when they are together in church that the preacher can apply the resources of the gospel to the deep issues in the lives of the people. This can be done with pastoral concern and a teacher's insight in the context of worship which conveys overtones of deeper meanings. And there is only one place where all of this can happen for most church members—the Sunday services.

Personal experience supports such an observation. For more than seventeen years, I had the privilege of serving one of the strongest congregations in our denomination. Among the congregation were persons of great talent and leadership, which they freely shared in the life of the church. Over the years—literally for more than a decade—we tried every method of adult education and group work available to us. No matter how hard we tried, each constituent program only reached about five percent of our congregation. Different groups participated in different programs; so in our combined efforts we may have reached ten to twenty percent of our people. On a weekly basis the percentage could drop even lower, since some of the programs were only occasional. However, on Sunday mornings, week after week, year in and year out, thirty-five to forty percent of our members would be in church, plus a good many other persons. For most of them, Sunday service was their only effective contact with the church.

Don't say it ought not to be that way. That's the way it is in most churches in the country. And the implication seems quite clear. The primary opportunity for communication in the church is the Sunday service. The minister's primary means of communicating with the people is the sermon which is offered to the gathered congregation.

Let me clarify this claim by pointing out what I am not saying. I am not talking about communicating the gospel outside the church. That is a quite different issue and requires different treatment. What is being affirmed here is the centrality of preaching as a means of communication in the church. The sermon is the minister's primary opportunity of communicating with the congregation. If we were to ask how to address the world outside the church, we should have to find other means and other occasions, because those people are not in church.

Also we are not talking about preaching in isolation from other aspects of the church's life. Preaching always occurs in a context: first of all the context of worship, then the context of the total ministry of the church. Preaching does not—cannot—carry the whole burden of communication. It is part of a network of opportunities designed to enrich and deepen the life and work of the church.

Laity and Clergy Together

A second presupposition underlies the present inquiry: *If there is to be any significant improvement in the quality of preqching, both lay and clergy must help it happen.* This may come as a surprise to laity and may be difficult for clergy to admit, but it is unavoidably true.

Laypersons may ask, "What on earth do we have to do with the quality of preaching? Isn't that what we pay the preacher for?"

Well, yes, but it is not quite so simple. The renewal of preaching depends on the participation of the laity as well as the work of the clergy.

A basic fact is that how a congregation receives a sermon is probably as important as how a preacher delivers it. We all know that the qualities of openness, expectancy, receptivity are essential to communication—on both sides of the pulpit.

Equally important is a shared understanding of what happens in preaching. A congregation that is informed about the central concerns of Christian faith and life is better equipped to enter into a serious consideration of these matters. When the congregation is sensitive to what happens in communication, they can be more receptive to what is being communicated. (*Being receptive* does not mean "agreeing with," but rather "grasping the meaning of.") If the members of the congregation have some understanding of what the preacher has gone through, in order to be ready to present a sermon, they may be able to receive it with imagination and expectancy.

Beyond this basic consideration, however, there are two immediately practical ways in which laypersons can contribute to the effectiveness of preaching. Preachers need two assurances which only the laity can give: (1) Laypeople really want to hear effective preaching; (2) Congregations will support their ministers in the disciplines which good preaching requires. Let's look at these two observations.

• Preachers need the assurance that laypeople really want to hear good sermons. Many ministers have been persuaded that preaching is not a good means of either communication or teaching, and there is considerable evidence that this may be true. So if you laypersons believe that effective preaching is, or could be, important, you must find ways of saying this so that preachers can hear it.

Saying it may be a little awkward. I am not asking you to promise to agree with everything you hear. Nor am I suggesting that you tell the preacher what to preach or what not to preach. What is proposed is more modest but more significant. Try to find ways of saying, "Pastor, one of the reasons we come to church is because we feel the need for thoughtful, helpful preaching. Your sermons are important to our religious life." You may think this should be obvious, but it is not. Either as personal friends or as official leaders in the church, affirm the value you put on effective preaching.

Hearing this may be equally awkward. We ministers have a tendency to be defensive about our sermons. The discussion of preaching may sound to us like criticism of what we are doing. (It may indeed be, but we will be more receptive if it does not sound like it.) We need a measure of personal and professional maturity to be able to hear what is being said.

• There is a second assurance which only the laity can give the clergy: Laity will support ministers in whatever disciplines are required for good preaching.

Effective preaching is hard work. And the hardest work is not what is visible in the sanctuary but the long, intense, private hours of preparation that are never seen by the congregation.

Creative preaching requires the investment of the minister's best hours and energies in this private labor. All ministers know this, to their discomfort. They also know that there are many other congregational and community needs which require their attention, and it is often difficult to know what to put first. That is why laypersons can help by saying to the minister, "Put sermon preparation at the top of your list of priorities, and we will support you in your decision."

Every time I talk with ministers about these matters, I recommend devoting their mornings to private creative work. Frequently they respond, "My congregation wouldn't let me get away with that. They expect me to be available at every moment." This means that many clergy are denying themselves the disciplines essential to creative preaching, because they think they must answer the phone or the doorbell every time it rings or be available for conversation at any time of day.

I doubt that this interpretation of what laypeople want and expect is accurate. But only laity can tell clergy whether they want instant response at all times or good preaching. If you want imaginative, helpful preaching, you must support your minister's commitment to the concentrated task of preparing for Sunday's sermon.

I believe that laypersons will gladly give such support. During the past couple of years, I have had the opportunity to test this belief with several groups. In every instance, they have stated their conviction that preaching is important. And recognizing the disciplines required for good preaching, they have affirmed their willingness to support their preachers in giving top priority to that task. Such assurance is necessary to sustain the clergy in their commitment to the work of preaching.

2
Sizing Up the Situation

It is true that one of the encouraging signs in the churches is a renewed interest in preaching. However, I quickly add a word of caution: We must not look for any immediate or dramatic change. The issues confronting us are serious, deep-rooted, long-standing. Any improvement will come only out of sustained commitment to excellence in preaching. If this sounds rather sober, I don't mind. The facts are indeed sobering, and change will come only as a result of an honest dealing with them.

If our concern for preaching is to have any significant influence in the church, it must be grounded in a thorough understanding of where we are and how we arrived here. Uninformed hope can only lead to false expectations and then to disillusionment. An informed hope may be less high-spirited, but it will be more sustaining. If we expect quick solutions to long-standing problems, we will be disappointed. But if we take full measure of the issues which confront us, we know what to expect and what to work for. So I invite you to a realistic diagnosis of the condition of preaching, so that we may engage in a serious effort at renewal.

The trouble with preaching is not just a casual or recent development. It did not come upon us in the seventies or the sixties or the fifties. The first fact which we must face is that the trouble with preaching is a problem of long standing.

We could amuse ourselves with quotations which reflect the poor quality of most sermons throughout most of the history of the church. What is more important for us, however, is to recognize that in American Protestantism preaching has been in decline for several decades. I will not put a date on it; let us say for half a century.

In the judgment of a sensitive American historian, "by the second quarter of the twentieth century the word 'preacher' had been shorn of much of its former dignity. The American Protestant ministry knew a kind of Indian summer in the opening years of the new century, but by about 1925 a winter of discontent had settled down upon it. 'Preacher' . . . was now a word without grandeur." [1]

The same author cites a sermon in 1930, delivered by one of America's great preachers, entitled "The Foolishness of Preaching." It was a defense of preaching but was addressed to "the arguments advanced to prove that the 'pulpit is an anachronism in the modern world' and that preaching is indeed foolishness." [2] I could note similar arguments from the 1940s and the 1950s and even from the 1920s. It all adds up to a half century of challenging the relevance of preaching.

Now I ask you to press this observation still deeper: *The trouble with preaching is rooted in the religious condition of our civilization and the theological condition of our churches.* Frankly, I do not know of any discussion of preaching which deals seriously with these matters. This may mean that the analysis is quite wrong; let me present it and you can judge for

18

yourself. There are three characteristics of our present religious condition, all of which bear on the trouble with preaching.

Religious Drift

Our American way of life is a part of Western civilization. What happens to that total civilization happens to America too—differently perhaps but unavoidably. One of the deepest and most pervasive characteristics of Western civilization and therefore of America is its basic secularism.

This may be a little hard for American church people to discern, because our churches are flourishing and there is even a popular style of American religion. But the deeper currents of our civilization have been drifting toward secularism, and it is these deep-moving currents which determine the direction our way of life actually takes.

Secularism simply means that the reality of God is less and less important to more and more people. Secularism is a religion without a deity. Its "god," at best, is humanity or human values. At a popular level, it may mean just getting by and enjoying life. At its least attractive, it becomes sheer self-interest and self-indulgence. All three varieties exist at the same time, side by side.

What we must understand is that the drift toward secularism has been the deepest intellectual mark of modern Western civilization, and that the process has been developing for at least two hundred years. The intellectual movement that shaped the modern mind was the Enlightenment, which swept through Europe and England during the eighteenth century. An article in a current news magazine speaks of the modern person as "a child of the Enlightenment." Whether we recognize our parentage or not, the identification is accurate. One of the ablest historians of this movement calls it "The Rise of Modern Paganism."[3] He is right. The growth of a new paganism (trust in science, politics, and other human achievements) gives primary place to humanistic or secular values. The other side of this is the decline of historic Christianity and its affirmation of God's graces, which indeed are the ultimate bases of human values.

Many church people may not be aware of this drift, even though the intellectual community takes it for granted. Popular religion has prospered in the United States, but more deeply, secularism has prevailed. As I write these lines, for instance, the most influential books dealing with such issues as love and marriage or even death and dying are books without the slightest Christian orientation. These questions were once deeply related to religious faith, but now the secular interpretation is widely accepted as authoritative even among church leaders.

There may be signs that secularism is going bankrupt. Some of my ablest colleagues say it is, and I would like to believe them. However, this would not change our understanding of where we are right now and how we arrived here.

What has this to do with preaching? A great deal. In such a religious climate, preaching will have trouble. This will be true, not because preachers are less capable than in former days, but because the general secular attitude does not encourage and support serious preaching. The problem is not the decline of preaching, but the growth of secularism and the resultant decline of conventional organized Christianity.

Preachers must take these factors into account in their self-understanding. Laity must be aware of the condition of our civilization if they are to understand what is happening in the churches.

Theological Uncertainty

The churches cannot be unaffected by such a religious drift; they must reckon with it. In fact, the churches have tried to address the rival religion of secularism in many ways. The resulting theological uncertainty is the second dimension of our current religious condition.

A vigorous evangelistic fervor marked the American churches during the nineteenth century, and yet this was the very period in which secularism was subtly infiltrating our way of life. The two movements occurred side by side. In some ways, the more obvious was the revivalist movement; it swept across the continent and resulted in the remarkable growth of the churches. More pervasive, however, and more sustained was the intellectual movement which dominated the life of colleges and universities. Ironically, many of these institutions were established by the churches.

Churches and movements with their roots in the revivalist tradition are still flourishing in our country, and they are an important factor in our religious life. It is my impression, however, that revivalistic Christianity does not try to reckon seriously with the religious drift which shapes our civilization.

On the other hand, many preachers and teachers have tried to relate the Christian message to the secular mind. This is a necessary and difficult task. One result has been a bewildering variety of interpretations of what Christianity really is. Indeed, in their effort to address modern secular persons, some teachers seem willing to surrender just about everything that is distinctively Christian. There are those who say we cannot affirm anything which is unacceptable to the modern secular mind. But the central convictions of our faith will never be acceptable to the modern secular mind. So do we surrender what we believe? Our other alternative is to acknowledge that there are differences, even conflicts, and try to engage in dialogue with people of secular beliefs. Almost every solution has been tried, resulting in confusing and even contradictory teachings, all in the name of Christianity.

One of the most gifted teachers of my own generation described the present period of theological thought as "between the times": "We live between the time of the theology which no longer makes sense to us and the time of a theology which has not yet clearly dawned." He added what seems to me a striking confession: "Theology written in this time between the times will not only be modest, it will be confused."[4] That was written in 1967, and although the intervening years have seen promising developments, I think the judgment is still sound.

An objective student of American thought may react sympathetically to such an evaluation. But what of the preachers? We have to preach next Sunday morning. We can't wait for theological clarity to dawn. And what of Christian believers? We have to cope with tomorrow, and we need an adequate faith right now.

Several things happen in our churches as a result of such theological uncertainty. In congregations I served over the past three decades, there were many well-educated persons. Although they were devoted to the church, many were quite uncertain what they could believe concerning God and even less clear what to think about Jesus. Most of them had long since discarded the orthodox faith they had inherited and had not found any convincing alternative.

How had they come to this point of troubled uncertainty while staying in the church? All the secular doubts had been raised in the university, and an array of unclear alternatives had been offered in the church. Consequently, they were not sure what to believe, although they were still persuaded that the church has some useful place in society.

Let me put it another way. One of the ablest of the new studies of preaching identifies "eight distinct alternatives" in current theological thought.[5] Each has its own strengths, and all are interpreted as viable options for Christians to choose. I accept the description as entirely accurate, but what happens to preaching in this context? Preachers themselves may switch from one alternative to another or hesitate among them. Consider the congregations who, in the course of their years of church attendance, may be exposed to several alternatives by successive preachers. What are they to believe?

This confusion is probably the reason why many laypersons have decided that theology is only for the scholars. As for themselves, church people are likely to settle for something else. Some say, "Let's just try to practice the golden rule." Others tackle social issues. Others seek ways of getting in touch with their own feelings. And in every option, the full meaning of the gospel can be compromised. As a consequence, many people never experience—never even hear about—the deeper possibilities of Christian living.

Now note: The essential issue here is not what is happening to preaching but what is happening to our faith. Confusion as to what we believe can only weaken the effectiveness of preaching. The preacher who is not sure what he believes cannot preach very persuasively. Somewhere I have read a lovely but sad statement about a mournful evangelist who had managed to misplace his gospel. You can guess what happens to preaching under those conditions. Similarly, I would suppose that church members who are uncertain of their faith will not expect much from equally uncertain preachers. In both instances, the problem is not simply with preaching but with the underlying beliefs. Preaching is ineffective, in part, because faith is confused.

Professional Identity Crisis

It is small wonder that in such a climate of religious drift and theological uncertainty many members of the clergy have experienced a professional identity crisis (the third dimension of our condition). They feel that they are given little support in our civilization. Their theology lacks clarity and assurance. Consequently, many clergy wonder who they are and what they are supposed to be doing. If our civilization questions the traditional ministries of the church, what are ministers to do? If theology questions the historic affirmations of faith, what are ministers to teach?

As a result, many clergy settle for a diminished understanding of their role. Some specialize in psychological counseling—it surely is helpful to enable people to get in touch with their feelings. Some concentrate on trying to change the structures of society, and there is biblical encouragement for this. Some seem content to tend the institution—for whatever good purposes it serves.

In any case, preaching suffers. Such personal and professional insecurity comes out in a person's preaching. As a perceptive professor of communication theory puts it: "The communication of the preacher's disbelief is subtle but potent. The preacher who lacks confidence in his role and in the efficacy of the spoken word, communicates his doubt by gesture, by intonation, and frequently by an obvious lack of adequate preparation."[6] And the question I am urging is not simply what is the matter with preaching. The basic questions are what is happening in our civilization, what is happening in our religion, and what effect is all this having on us in our churches.

3
The Challenge to Preaching

There is another aspect of the present condition of preaching which must be brought into the open. It relates to the professional training of the clergy, and it is a situation about which the laity ought to be informed.

It has already been suggested that many ministers are quite uncertain whether preaching really has any value. Perceptive laypersons, on hearing this, perhaps for the first time, might well ask where the clergy ever picked up the notion that sermons are not an important means of communication. The answer has to be their professional training. Such a response may come as a surprise to the laity; so let me state the claim rather simply and directly. Then, before anyone, lay or clergy, reacts too strongly, let me clarify it with some care.

For the past thirty-five years in the professional training of the clergy, the importance of preaching has been widely and seriously disputed and frequently denied.

This is an impressionistic judgment; it is based on personal observations. I have no desire to document it in detail. You can believe that it would hardly be questioned in academic theological circles. Countless ministers have said to me that in seminary they had little or no training in preaching, and they are graduates of many different schools.

Whenever I speak of this to the laity, they respond with astonished disbelief. They find it hard to accept that the professional education of the clergy may include only minimal, and perhaps even no, specific training in the art of preaching. When they see that I am serious, they can only express their dismay. Most laypersons do not know this, and most clergy do not talk about it. However, we can understand the present state of preaching only by knowing and measuring these facts. That is why I am venturing to tell it as I think it is and to invite both laity and clergy, both congregations and educators, to hear each other.

Now let me state the claim somewhat more carefully. It is not that *all* theological schools and *all* teachers have denied the importance of preaching. Happily, in some schools the teaching of preaching has been highly regarded, and preaching has always had its champions among the teachers of clergy.

But—and this is the important fact—over the past few decades in many theological schools, preaching has not been considered a particularly important subject for serious study. And in many, perhaps most, schools there have been able, respected teachers who have seriously and persuasively challenged or denied the importance of preaching as a part of the ministerial task.

Why do I say thirty-five years? Because that is the length of time during which I have had direct personal contact with theological education. And the demeaning or discrediting of preaching has been one continuing aspect of theological education during that time. I know this, because, along with others, I have opposed the trend with (until recent years) discouraging results.

When I was in seminary, there were those who argued persuasively that not preaching but personal counseling is the primary task of the professional minister. At about the same time, we were assured by some that what really matters is the church's concern for political and economic reform. Later, the clergy's role was given a somewhat different emphasis, namely, enlisting in community organizations and working for the radical restructuring of society. During the past decade or so, it has been asserted that communication theory demonstrates preaching to be an outmoded means of communication which should be replaced by something more appropriate to our electronic age. So it has gone for thirty years, and all these emphases still continue side by side, in fact, all mixed up with one another. You can imagine the cumulative unsettling effects of all the turmoil.

I remember very well a long evening's conversation at least twenty years ago with members of a theological faculty. Almost to a person, they contended that preaching cannot be taught anyway. So why take it so seriously? Train the student thoroughly in theology, biblical studies, ethics, psychology, social sciences, they said, and surely the student will be able to put it all together. He will be able to deliver it in presentable bits and pieces for Sunday sermons.

I suggested that these professors were persons of unusual gifts who were indeed able to organize and illuminate their beliefs and commitments in persuasive form. In their own education, they had probably had some good teachers of public speaking. However, most of us are persons of ordinary gifts. There is no guarantee that we become good public speakers through undergraduate studies. Besides, preaching is a rather special craft, which is not ordinarily taught at the college level. Therefore, I urged that the teaching of preaching deserves a significant place in the curriculum of the theological school.

Twenty years ago (indeed, thirty or ten) those of us who championed such a view did not prevail. I say this not to complain or to point a finger but to identify a fact.

"But," you may ask, "isn't it different now? Isn't it true that, as of now, there is a greater acceptance of the importance of preaching?"

Yes, and it is a welcome change. But we cannot overlook three or four decades of history. Something happened during those years that cannot be easily or quickly erased. Let me explain.

• The suspicion that preaching may be unimportant is a self-fulfilling prophecy. Once ministers seriously suspect that their preaching may be unimportant, that is exactly what it becomes—unimportant. The reason for this fact is terrifyingly simple.

Preparing a sermon is hard work. Indeed, it is the peculiar kind of hard work that one is easily tempted to put aside. There are always other tasks, which are simpler, more pressing, and may even appear more important. Ministers, like everybody else, have only a limited supply of time and energy, which they will invest in what they consider to be the most immediate and relevant tasks. Therefore, if ministers begin to think that preaching may not be important, they will set aside the task of sermon preparation and turn to the more pressing and apparently productive tasks, like administration or pastoral care. Minimal attention will be given to the sermon; since, after all, it is not required until Sunday. This work can be done at some other time, usually under last-minute pressure.

Such treatment of sermon preparation soon begins to show up in the sermon itself. This is the strange irony; because preachers suspect sermons may not be particularly significant, they avoid the very disciplines that are necessary if preaching is to be effective. And the decline in the quality of their preaching soon becomes noticeable to everyone.

There is evidence that many preachers are uneasy with this condition. They suspect that sermons ought to be important but fear they are not. But they have no motivation to invest themselves in the work of preaching, because they have been persuaded that it is an ineffective means of communication.

• Now note what happens as the years pass. The effect of this suspicion is cumulative, not only in the personal life of the preacher, but in the total life of the church.

28

Every year the schools of theology graduate a new generation of ministers. In each generation, there is a significant number of persons who have been persuaded that preaching is not an important aspect of the ministry. There are others who are not quite sure what they think about preaching. Then, in the parish, they are confronted by the hard demands of sermon preparation and the many-sided opportunities of other aspects of their ministry. Many of them gradually cut back on the time given to study and sermon preparation and spend their best energies and hours at other tasks.

Now multiply these annual generations by my estimate of thirty-five years. Imagine how many ministers there are presently serving churches who are uncertain about the importance of preaching in their ministries. Consequently, they do not give sermon preparation the time and work it requires, and, therefore, they are increasingly insecure in their preaching. Some ministers are aware of this problem but not certain how to handle it. Others, unfortunately, seem quite unaware of it or unwilling to talk about it. In any case, the laity can only wonder what is wrong. Perhaps now you can understand my concern about our situation.

At a recent meeting of professors of preaching, there was unanimous agreement that there is a bright, new interest in preaching among theological students. I share the enthusiasm for such a welcome development but see in it no possibility of significant change in the current life of the church. It will be ten or twenty years before this year's graduates have achieved positions of influence and leadership in the churches. What do we do in the meantime? The problem is now, and we must deal with it now.

I am urging that first we take full measure of the circumstances in which we are involved, see them in all their complexity and depth, and recognize that we are dealing with a serious, deep-rooted, long-developing condition. If you find all this as sobering as I do and are willing to commit yourself to an earnest confrontation with the issues, then you are ready to ask what we may reasonably hope to achieve.

4

A Well-Tempered Hope

What we can honestly hope for must be defined in terms of the complex religious conditions of our time. We must start from where we are, not where we would like to think we are. The issues of the present give direction to the possibilities of the future. The dimensions of our religious situation give shape to our expectations. So let me state our hope in terms of the three basic issues, which we have identified.

True Expectations

If America has experienced the religious drift I outlined, we must be realistic in our expectations. We must not expect even the most effective renewal of preaching to produce a quick transformation of our national life. If Western civilization is as thoroughly secularized as some say it is, any significant change will require more than a squadron of committed clergy.

Many ministers and church members are disillusioned about the church and its ministries, because they expect too much. Preachers are often discouraged, because their sermons do not result in the conversion of their congregations to the preacher's own persuasions. But this is to expect too much of sermons—or indeed of any combination of programs. Laypersons are often discouraged because they imagine that if more people would come to church and could hear better sermons, the ills of society would soon be cured. If our society is as secularized as has been suggested, something far more radical and far-reaching is required.

Our expectations for a renewal of preaching must be modest. I see the central task of the church as keeping alive the Christian option in every generation and in every civilization. We can work for the implementation of this option. But in a civilization as widely pluralistic as ours, perhaps the most we can hope for is to inject the Christian witness into the welter of options among which people can choose. And in a civilization as deeply secular as ours, perhaps the most we can hope for is that the witness will be heard. Whether it will be accepted is quite another matter, which is beyond our power to guarantee.

Far from incidentally, this task of the church in society is not the work of the clergy alone or even primarily. It is the work of the laity. They are the ones who are "out there" in a sense in which ministers cannot be. The role of the clergy is basically to help laity find the Christian resources with which to do God's work in the world.

Doing Theology

The most important task of minister and congregation, then, is to *do theology* in their local church. To do theology means to think about and to understand what we believe and how that faith relates to our daily lives. It also means to

31

discover and appropriate the resources of faith which enable us to live effectively. This is what the minister and people accomplish together in the local congregation.

If it is true that our way of life is deeply infected by secularism, we need to consider in sermon and study just what is happening and how we may relate to it. If we are called to keep alive the Christian option, we had better know what that option is and what it demands of us who affirm it. This is what preaching and teaching are all about.

In these matters, professional theologians have an important role to play, and clergy have the responsibility of knowing what the scholars are doing and interpreting it for congregations. However, the task of doing theology is also the work of a local congregation, minister and people together. The primary place to do theology is the local parish, where we all are engaged in the anguish and joy of life. What we believe comes alive in the local congregation and in the life of the congregation in society.

So ministers find their identity as *enablers*—to use the current term—or as "helpers of your joy," which is the way Paul expressed it (II Cor. 1:24, KJV). Laypersons find their identity as members of the body of Christ, drawing sustenance from their life together in the congregation and doing God's work in the world.

The Primacy of Preaching

Preaching is of central importance in this congregational task. Yet, it must also be said that preaching is related to all the other aspects of the life and work of a congregation.

Sunday worship is the only time when most of us gather together to deal with matters of ultimate importance. As one of our nation's outstanding teachers of preachers observes, "At the time of the sermon the vast majority of the people in our particular corner of Western civilization encounter their only systematic exposure to any kind of reflection on the meaning of things."[1] This is surely correct. Sunday after Sunday we come to church to open ourselves to God, to find some strength and guidance for our lives, to see if there is any healing for our secret hurts, and to give a hand to others who are also seeking. Everything that happens in church may work to these ends, but central to the occasion is the interpretation of the gospel as it may be understood and experienced in our life together.

Clearly, this means that the preacher must come to the service out of a time of serious preparation. Is there an equivalent kind of preparation with which the people may come to church? I suspect there is—at least, a spirit of expectancy, an openness to hear, a willingness to learn and grow.

Then what we do in church must be related to what we do all week long. In order for this to happen, most of us need more time together than a twenty-minute sermon or an hour of worship. So the church provides other occasions, the pastor offers other ministries. We gather as learners, as inquirers, as sharers of common experiences, as supporters of one another. And preaching finds its place in a network of congregational experiences.

As we do theology together in church, we go forth to do God's work in the world. The impact on our national way of life may not be immediately noticeable. Indeed, we cannot be sure what will happen to our civilization. But God's work of communicating his word is done: first in church, then in daily life; first by clergy, then by laity.

Dare we hope this much? Dare we engage in the implementing of this hope?

A Thesis

Our common participation in the preaching and hearing of sermons is basic to the realization of such hope, and it is this experience that you are invited to consider in the present study. There is a two-sided thesis which will give shape to the inquiry. It may be helpful to state it here so we may anticipate the direction of the discussion.

• *Preaching is a communicative event.* That is, a sermon is an occasion when people come together in the context of corporate worship to engage in the communication and celebration of the gospel. What happens depends on how the sermon is preached and how it is heard. Communication is likely to be most effective when we, congregation as well as preacher, understand how communication between persons actually takes place.

• *Preaching is also a creative event.* That is, the work of communication is basically a creative task. A sermon must be treated like a work of art—modest, perhaps, but nonetheless art. The preacher must bring to the task of preaching the same creative skills that are exercised in any comparable art. The congregation must use the same gifts of imagination and receptivity that they bring to the appreciation of any comparable art.

The communication of the gospel calls for creativity in both preacher and congregation. If we can learn about communication and creativity, we may be able to experience more deeply the full meaning of the gospel.

PART 2

PREACHING AS COMMUNICATIVE EVENT

5
An Acoustical Affair

What actually happens when we try to communicate with each other? This is an urgent question about a fascinating and fundamental human experience.

The importance of communication is so obvious that we often take it for granted. We must communicate with each other; it is part of our being human. Our relationships with one another depend on this capacity.

One of the most painful phrases in our vocabulary is "the failure to communicate" or "a breakdown in communication." Tension and conflict are often attributed to such failure. Sometimes we cannot get through to each other, and our relationships are damaged. On the other hand, our joys and successes are dependent upon the effectiveness of our communication with one another.

But what actually happens when we try to communicate?

What enables communication to succeed? What gets in the way? What is going on inside us, between us, among us, when we communicate with one another?

The Development of Communication Theory

During the past thirty years, there has been an enormous development in this whole field of study. Communication theory has grown into an extensive academic discipline. Beginning rather modestly in the 1940s, it has not only amassed an impressive body of knowledge in its own right but has become extensively interrelated with many other academic studies. The bibliography in communication theory is immense.

One collection of essays includes contributions from representatives of ten different disciplines, all of them seriously concerned with how we communicate with one another.[1] Another author claims that the preparation of his book "required a systematic review of over one hundred scientific journals, a survey of some 100,000 titles, and a working bibliography of 6,000 articles."[2]

Obviously, I cannot claim to have mastered such an extensive subject. My own bibliography lists a mere fourteen volumes, which have been studied in preparation for this present work. Another dozen or so have been looked at and set aside. I have consulted with colleagues regarding which works have impressed or helped them and have received quite different answers from each one. So any scholar can point to gaps in my bibliography, but I believe it is representative of works in the field.

There are several approaches to the study of communication. We who are not experts ought to recognize this. There are differences of outlook and interpretation among communication theorists themselves. So we must be careful not to make broad generalizations about what communication theory says. There are basic agreements, but there are also important differences among students in this field.

One basic approach is empirical. In such studies, the attempt is made to measure, to quantify, all the elements in communication. Another approach is more reflective, perhaps even philosophical. In these works, consideration is given to the meaning of the process itself and of the human beings involved. Some students try to combine the empirical and the reflective approaches. They suggest—wisely, it seems to me—that there may be some elements in human experience that cannot easily be measured, and measurement, even when possible, may not exhaust meaning. Empirical exactness and thoughtful reflection make a good combination in the study of human communication.

Obviously, much of this work is likely to be relevant to the hearing and preaching of sermons. But there are two qualifications to be kept in mind. First, not all empirical studies are of equal importance to our specific concern. We may have to exercise some judgment at this point. Second, let's be unashamedly eclectic. We need not become attached to any one school of thought; we may learn from everybody.

I cannot resist adding one observation which impresses me as being both amusing and ironic. In order to engage in this study, I had to learn a new vocabulary, the specialized language of communication theory. Treatises on this subject are generally very difficult to read. As an academic discipline, communication theory has developed its own specialized vocabulary which must be translated into ordinary language. That is what I will try to do in the next discussion, hoping that not too much is lost in translation.

The Communication Explosion

The development of communication theory took place largely on the campuses of our universities in laboratories and classrooms. That is why some of us were not as aware as we might have been of the important discoveries being made. But at the same time, there occurred a *communication explosion,* which none of us could miss. It was happening right in our living rooms. In bewildering profusion, mass media have multiplied during the past quarter century. Radio, magazines, newspapers, and TV have assaulted our senses with amazing power and variety. Some of the best talents of our time, funded with apparently limitless financial resources, are dedicated to the not always noble arts of manipulation and persuasion. Small wonder that serious students of communication theory speak of an *information explosion,* or communication explosion, and of *total immersion* in a welter of *input overload.*

All of this makes more difficult the modest communication efforts of the church and particularly of preaching. First of all, the competition for attention is enormous. The multiplication of words being uttered makes it difficult for us to pay attention to them. We have to tune out some in order to hear any. Moreover, the voices are persuasive, the methods clever, and preachers cannot always match the competition.

In addition to this general observation, there are two serious consequences of the communication explosion as they reflect on preaching: the reduced value of words and our skeptical attitude as listeners.

One of the results of the growth of communication through mass media has been what one preacher rightly calls "a serious devaluation of our verbal currency."[3] That is, many of the cleverest efforts at communication are commercially motivated. Their persuasive earnestness is an act designed to sell us something. Words are used in order to manipulate us—and we know it. As a consequence, the integrity of language is destroyed. Words do not necessarily mean what they say. The real peril may be that we have learned to live with dishonesty and to accept it as an everyday fact.

One thoughtful observer comments: "Words are trifles, to most men. They have heard them too often. It is all fake, advertising, propaganda, lying. Indeed it is. But why is there so much abuse of language? Only important things are imitated and abused and perverted. . . . The corruption of the best is worse than any other."[4] But words are the preacher's primary tool. What happens when our principal means of communication is cheapened, abused, rendered suspect?

One effect can be observed at the other end of the process. Precisely because of the dishonest use of words, many of us listen to everything with an attitude of suspicion and skepticism. How can I know that you really mean what you say? Are you simply trying to manipulate me? So when preachers step into the pulpit to put a sermon into words, the members of the congregation may already have their guard up.

Whether the context of worship reduces the level of skepticism is a question I cannot answer. We might hope so, but only the laity really knows. In any case, we all realize that the communication explosion has made infinitely more difficult the task of preaching and hearing sermons.

"Faith Comes by Hearing"

We who are concerned about preaching, whether as preachers or hearers, must function in a rich but puzzling time. There are many helps for our task and many hindrances to it. It may be that the task of communication has never been so complicated. This means that learning how to hear a message and learning how to make it hearable may be as important today as it ever has been in the history of Christianity. This is certainly true if, as Paul sugggested, "faith comes by hearing" (Rom. 10:17). In commenting on this statement, Martin Luther put it differently: "Faith is an acoustical affair." Both statements have interested me for a long time, and they are relevant to us at this point in our discussion.

After suggesting that "faith comes by hearing," Paul added, "hearing" comes by "words." If I may trust my limited knowledge of Greek, the term that Paul used was not *preaching* (in the usual sense of proclamation). The Greek term means *words,* which I would venture to interpret as witnessing. What Paul said is profoundly related to what we are concerned with in this inquiry. *We can only believe what we hear, and hearing depends on how we listen and on how the message is expressed.*

In other words, our religious faith and experience depend on the process of communication. Therefore, we would be wise to learn all we can about this process. If faith comes by hearing, we must learn to listen. But hearing depends not only on how we listen, but on how well the words convey the message. So we would be wise to learn how to send a communication. What really happens when we try to put our message into words?

Because faith comes by hearing, and hearing by words, the quality of our religious experience depends on our ability to communicate with one another. That's what communication theory is all about.

6
Communication Theory and Preaching

Before undertaking an analysis of the process of communication, I would like to offer a few general observations about the relation between the academic discipline itself and the actual practice of preaching. This is necessary, because there seems to be a rather widespread opinion that communication theory tends to discredit preaching. Add to this the common observation that conventional forms of preaching may be rendered obsolete by the new media. Both of these affirmations are quite familiar among the clergy. They add up to an uneasy suspicion that there may be some conflict between communication theory and preaching and that preachers should face up to reality. If the laity are not aware of this uneasiness, they should know that many clergy labor under such insecurity.

I should like to dispel this suspicion at the beginning of our study of communication theory. It is a misinterpretation of the facts. Let me state my conviction quite directly, and then develop it further.

A Valued Ally

Communication theory does not discredit preaching as a means of communication. Communication theory is, in fact, a valuable ally of preaching.

Frankly, this discovery came as a surprise. Over the past decade or so, I had picked up the clear impression that scientific studies affirm quite convincingly that preaching is a poor means of communication. These conclusions were always stated in the name of communication theory or learning theory, and they were always labeled scientific or empirical. So those of us who were unacquainted with the actual studies took seriously the judgments offered by those who seemed to be better informed.

Consequently, I began the study of communication theory somewhat defensively, fully expecting to run into much negative material. To my surprise and delight, I found just the opposite: communication theory provides a great resource of insight and understanding which can be most helpful to preaching.

The scientific study of communication does, indeed, disclose how complex and difficult the process is. The analysis of what actually happens in communication reveals the enormous obstacles which must be overcome. Comparative studies indicate clearly that different methods of communication are effective in different ways, and that we should choose our method in relation to what we want to accomplish. A lecture, for instance, does not communicate in the same way as a small group discussion, and vice versa. We should know the difference.

So it is true that communication theory helps us see the limits of public address, the hazards and difficulties that lie in the process. But in all this there is nothing to discredit preaching. Rather, the theory offers us knowledge which enables us to improve our means of communication, including preaching.

What has happened is that preachers and teachers of preaching have drawn inferences from communication theory that the theory itself does not necessarily imply. Let me illustrate this by relating an incident that still makes me grin when I think of it.

Some time ago, I was negotiating with an authority in communication theory to participate in a conference for preachers. Talking with him on the phone one day, I said that preachers needed to hear him affirm his support of preaching as a means of communication (he happens to be a stout advocate of preaching). I added, "You know that some of your colleagues in communication theory have persuaded a lot of preachers that preaching is no longer useful."

"Name one such colleague," he replied.

I hesitated a bit, and named one.

His quick rebuttal, delivered in a tone which emphasized every word was, *"He's your colleague, not mine!"*

What did he mean? He meant that the person whom I was citing was not an expert in communication theory but a clergyman who was drawing implications from what he knew about the subject. My friend meant further that the clergyman in question was jumping to conclusions which were not justified by the evidence.

This is what I meant earlier by suggesting that we be careful in drawing inferences from communication theory and applying them to preaching. We must recognize the extensiveness of the studies, the complexity of the data, and interpret them with great care.

It is obvious, of course, that I run the same risk of selecting only data which fit a prearranged conclusion. There is no way to avoid the risk; we can only take it as knowingly as possible and test our conclusions as honestly as possible. Based on an examination of representative writings in the field, I offer the judgment that communication theory is, or can be if we will master it, an important ally of preaching.

Communication theory can help us to understand what actually happens when we try to communicate with one another. The process has been studied exhaustively by every method that the scientific imagination has been able to devise. Communication proves to be far more difficult and complicated than we ordinarily suppose. Artists have known this intuitively. Scientists have analyzed it with precision. And we all will be the wiser for learning what artists and scientists have discovered. The preaching and hearing of sermons will be a more significant event when clergy and laity understand what is happening.

Of course, we do not need to be scientific experts to know that communication is difficult. I remember an occasion, at least thirty years ago, when this insight was expressed by Henry Hitt Crane, one of the most eloquent preachers of his generation. This is how he said it.

I stand before my congregation saying, "Blue, blue, blue."

They sit there thinking, "Yellow, yellow, yellow."

What they hear, then, is "Green, green, green."

Of course he was exactly right, but such intuitions may be deepened and enlarged by the discoveries of scientific study.

All preachers need to know that what they think they are saying is not necessarily what is being heard. All laypersons need to know that what they think they are hearing is not necessarily what the preacher is saying. If this sounds confusing, it is! But it is also true, and we need to know it. The encouraging fact is that by knowing it we can speak and hear more effectively. Scientific study has identified most of the obstacles to communication; they are found both in ourselves and in the process. Knowing what they are, we can either find our way around them or turn them to our advantage.

That is what communication theory can do for us. It is

surely an important resource for persons interested in preaching.

The Power of the Spoken Word

There is another important insight which is affirmed by some of the ablest students of human communication: *The spoken word carries a unique power, which distinguishes it from every other form of communication.* Human speech is our most important means of communicating with one another. It may be accompanied and supplemented by other forms: sights, sounds, nonverbal expressions. But basic to all, conveying the most significant meanings, is the spoken word.

Walter Ong is a man of broad and deep learning. His reflections on communication are always profound and often eloquent. He affirms with clarity and conviction the power of the spoken word. "Man communicates with his whole body, and yet the word is his primary medium. Communication, like knowledge itself, flowers in speech."[1] Marshall McLuhan, a man of equally massive learning, strengthens Ong's observation. "The spoken word involves all of the senses dramatically."[2]

Frank Dance is a scholar who draws together empirical study and philosophic reflection. He puts the matter quite simply, "The spoken word is central to man's communication."[3] And in a collection of studies that Dance edited, a professor of speech quotes a grammarian, "The spoken and heard word is the primary form for language, and of far greater importance than the secondary form used in writing [printing] and reading."[4]

It is significant that such strong agreement should be voiced by these men who approach human communication from several different directions. Ong states it eloquently: "The spoken word does have more power than the written to do what the word is meant to do, to communicate. . . . The

47

written medium simply will not tolerate all of what actually goes on in oral speech."[5]

Interestingly enough, these students also agree that the advent of electronic media of communication has intensified the power of spoken words. The media depend not only upon vision but upon hearing. They have increased the importance of sight and sound in our consciousness and sound every bit as much as sight. This is the clear implication of many of McLuhan's insights. Ong expresses it quite directly. He points out that there were centuries during which writing and printing were the principal means of mass communication. Then came electronics, and as Ong says, "Voice, muted by script and print, has come newly alive."[6]

The power of the spoken word lies in its capacity to reveal what is within a person. Words emerge from within one person and are addressed to the inner being of another person. Only speech can communicate in this extraordinary manner from one private self to another. I have heard Dance lecture on this aspect of human communication with an eloquence which embodies the assertion. In fact, it is difficult to write about the power of the spoken word. Something is lost in the transition. As a philosopher Ong must resort to almost poetic language to convey his meanings. "Sound is a special sensory key to interiority. . . . Sight reveals surfaces. Sound reveals the interior without the necessity of invasion. . . . Because the spoken word moves from interior to interior, encounter between man and man is achieved largely through voice."[7]

Building on these insights, Dance asserts that "the spoken word is an effective means of change." He supports his assertion by adding: "Evidence of this statement is available from reflection, anecdote, common sense, and experimentation. Work in verbal-conditioning, the psychology of propaganda, the rhetoric of agitation, and the functions of speech communication, all testify to the role of speech communication in changing attitudes and behavior."[8]

These affirmations have important implications for

preaching. Obviously, the spoken word occurs in many different relationships: intimate conversations, small groups, as well as public occasions such as corporate worship. But preaching is certainly one use of the spoken word. Any power that is implicit in human speech is capable of being exercised when words are shaped into a sermon.

One unique characteristic of the spoken word is also a distinctive mark of the sermon: it exists only at the moment of being spoken and heard. This is really a tantalizing thought. A sermon exists only at the instant in which it is being spoken by the preacher and heard by the congregation. Again it is Ong who says it best. "The spoken word cannot be reduced to space . . . it rides on time . . . it exists only at the moment of becoming and passing away! So the word is in a sense mystery."[9]

Thor Hall has reflected seriously on what these reflections may mean for preaching.[10] He concludes that the spoken word is "a more potent form of religious communication than any other medium I can think of."[11] The sermon, therefore, can be a most effective instrument for the communication of religious faith and experience.

In a sense more profound than Paul may have imagined, faith comes in the event of really hearing one another, and authentic hearing comes when words reveal the true person.

7
The Communicative Event

The Model

One of the favorite devices of communication theorists, and a very useful one, is to construct models of the communication process. These are attempts to portray the event in various forms which help us to see the process in different ways. The models range from rather simple to extremely complex. Simple models tend to miss some of the subtle aspects of human communication. Complex models run the risk of becoming too complicated, adding to the mystery of the process.

Naturally, I have tried my hand at model making. The result will win no prizes for brilliance or originality, but it may be useful. It is an attempt to visualize the communication process with special reference to the occasion of preaching and worship. Before presenting the model, I will identify the sources used. Then the model itself will be followed by an interpretation of its meaning. (In the final analysis, we always need words, don't we.)

THE COMMUNICATIVE EVENT
(A Model)

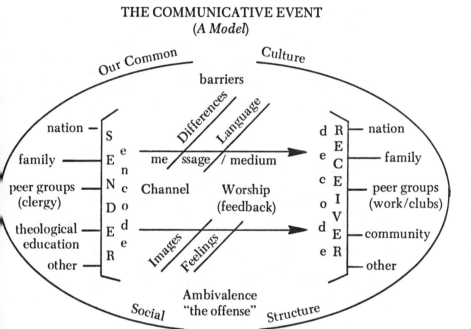

The simplest communication model is one of the earliest, the Shannon-Weaver Model. This can be found in almost every study of communication theory.[1] Because it is based primarily on mechanical or electronic devices, it is too simplistic to account for many factors in the human process. But it remains basic and will be reflected in my own model.

The attempt to account for human factors leads to the complexities of other models. Among these, and they are many, there is one which indicates the influence of various social groups on the participants. It is known as the Rickey Model.[2]

Another significant element in communication is the barriers which are encountered in the process. These are especially evident in the congregational situation. The clearest interpretation of these barriers I found in the model offered by Reuel Howe, the only one, incidentally, which relates specifically to preaching and worship.[3]

The basic form of my model has been drawn from these three sources, to which I have added a few observations growing out of parish experience. The result is intended to be a model which represents what happens when we come to church and listen to a preacher delivering a sermon.

What Happens in Communication?

Now let us interpret the model, trying to be quite specific about what actually happens when we humans communicate with one another. Perhaps I should add that there are some variations of vocabulary among communication theorists. The terms used in the model are representative. Remember also that our interpretation is related to the specific event of preaching and hearing a sermon.

THE PARTICIPANTS

The participants in communication are known as the sender and the receiver. In the church, of course, these are the preacher and the congregation (receiver in the plural).

The model represents one-to-one communication, and for visualization, this is useful. In church, of course, we are dealing with communication one-to-many (or at least several), and we must recognize at once that under this circumstance the process is complicated infinitely. Communication in a one-to-one relationship is difficult enough. But when we multiply the receivers by as many people as there are in the congregation (whether twenty or two thousand), the task becomes immeasurably more complex. Every factor in the process is multiplied by infinity. But before considering these elements, it will be helpful to look somewhat more carefully at the participants themselves (that is ourselves).

In every communication model which I have studied, it is interesting to note that the sender and the receiver are what we might call mirror images of each other. What happens at either end of the process is the reverse of the other. This is simply to say that we all are human beings and use the same human capacities in our relationships. But it adds the helpful insight that when we try to communicate with each other, we both (or all) are engaging in quite the same sort of activity. Inside ourselves, we look rather alike.

Sender and receiver(s) are influenced by many sociological factors, and the model indicates this. We share the same culture, and live in the same social structures. But beyond these common influences, differences begin to appear. Our family backgrounds are different. The social groups in which we participate are different. The peer groups who influence us are different. All these differences help to make us who we are, and we bring them with us to every occasion.

This is why I list theological education as one of the factors on the sender's side which does not figure on the receiver's side. The preacher's professional education generates real differences which complicate the communication process. On the other side, the special educational or cultural or vocational experiences of the laity inject their own complicating effect. We shall say more about all this later. But it is important right at the outset, while looking at the participants in communication (ourselves), to see both the common qualities and the distinctive differences which are influencing the process.

The preachers and lay members of the congregations bring every one of these factors to church with them. All of our likenesses and our differences work together in infinitely bewildering combinations to influence the way we preach and hear sermons.

THE PROCESS

The process is basically simple. The sender *encodes* the message, sends it along the *channel*, and the receiver *decodes* it. For our purposes, this means that a preacher designs a sermon, puts it into words, preaches it, and the congregation hears and interprets it. This seems simple enough, but the minute we read the sentence, we know that the process is extremely difficult and complicated.

The channel, it is important to note, is the entire service of worship. A sermon, properly speaking, never exists in isolation; it always occurs in the context of worship. The occasion, then, or *medium* (as the channel is sometimes called) is the whole liturgy.

The communication process begins the moment we enter the sanctuary and continues until we leave. (It may even be extended in both directions.) In church, then, it is dramatically true that, as some communication theorists neatly put it, "nothing never happens." This means that something is always happening and is part of the process of communication. Everything that occurs in church communicates something.

Preachers and congregations ought to be especially sensitive to this fact. The uneven candles, hastily lit at the last minute, the Scripture indifferently read, the halting sermon, the yawn, even the outside bulletin board—every one of these is saying something. And just to be fair, the well-read liturgy, the carefully prepared sermon, the attentive people, the clean steps into the church; these also communicate.

Some writers put it like this, "One cannot not communicate." Preachers who come to the service with a sense of its hope and promise, who express this in what they say and the way they say it, are sending significant messages. People who come to church with an air of friendliness and expectancy, not only receive the messages gracefully, but are themselves sending messages to one another. Both senders and receivers are enabling communication to happen more effectively.

It is frequently observed that communication is a two-way process. This is true in church too. Some critics of preaching portray it as a one-way attempt at communication, in which the members of the congregation are passive receivers. This is not really true; at least, if preacher and congregation know what preaching is all about, it need not be true. In any thoughtful design of a sermon, the congregation has already had significant input. Their needs, their joys, their crises have helped shape the sermon. But it is also true that a congregation can be active throughout the entire experience of worship. The people communicate with the preacher as they participate in the liturgy and receive the sermon. Indeed, they communicate with each other. In a congregation, communication is not only two-way; it proceeds in many directions at the same time.

THE PROBLEMS

The difficulties in communication become apparent when we reflect on all the complex factors in the process. The purpose of this section is to spell out these difficulties in some detail, but the intent is not at all negative. It is by looking honestly at the barriers to communication that we can deal with them and improve the effectiveness of the process itself.

There are all kinds of complications. Some are simply nuisances in the setting which can be removed or endured. There are differences among the people involved and indeed differences between clergy and laity. Most serious of all are the barriers within ourselves, laity and clergy alike, which make communication difficult. Let's look at these difficulties one by one. Our hope is that such an examination will enable us either to remove them or to put up with them or to render them less troublesome.

• There may be distractions in the occasion itself: misplaced furniture; awkward movements by the liturgist or preacher; the restlessness of children; the shuffling of choir or congregation; stale air, unchanged since a previous service or class meeting. People who are responsible for professional or commercial gatherings would be alert to such possible distractions. We should be too. Most of them can be relieved.

• Differences among members of the congregation are essential to the life of the church, but they certainly complicate the business of communication. Consider a typical congregation on a typical Sunday: the differences of age, of social position, of educational background, of political persuasion. How can a person hope to communicate with everybody in a group like that? Yet, it is precisely these differences which constitute one strength of the church. The church is not simply a group of congenial, like-minded people. It is a representative cross section of the community. If this complicates our life together in the church, it is not unlike our life in society. Such diversity is one of the assets of the church.

However, when we think of preaching a sermon to such a diverse group or calculating how so many different people will respond to a single sermon, the difficulty of communication in church becomes apparent. If ministers and members can be aware of this complexity, preachers will learn to preach better and hearers will learn to listen better. Sermons will be designed to communicate with different people. Individuals will receive the message according to their interests and concerns and recognize that others are receiving the message in their own ways.

• Differences between preachers and members of the congregation may act as barriers to communication. Two of these seem to be of particular importance.

There may be a difference of *image,* which is how we see ourselves and each other. Some preachers may regard themselves as authority figures to be listened to with respect, but members of the congregation may not see them that way at all. Or some people may expect their ministers to be ideal Christians, while the ministers themselves want to be accepted as fallible human beings, just like everybody else. Or we may swing back and forth from one image to another on different occasions.

More serious are our differences in *language* or in *understanding* the faith. Here the minister's professional training is an important factor. Ministers have necessarily learned the technical language of several disciplines: theology and biblical studies, sociology, psychology, education, philosophy. Not only vocabularies, but ways of thinking and believing are inevitably shaped by such training.

One way I sometimes illustrate this is to say that most preachers do not even read the Bible the same way most laypeople do. Most professional clergy have been trained in the literary and historical study of Scripture and have come to a rather refined understanding of its authority. Most laypersons have not been so trained and do not understand the authority of Scripture in this way. So we read the same Bible but read it differently. And these differences are reflected in what we put into sermons, as preachers, or hope to get out of them, as listeners.

To bridge such gaps in understanding is a very difficult task indeed, and they must be bridged from both directions. It is the task of the clergy to try to teach what they take to be authentic and adequate interpretations of the Christian faith. It is the task of the laity to try to learn what options are available to mature, well-informed Christians and choose what seems most helpful to them.

For instance, *redemption* is one of the great words of the Christian faith and one of the crucial experiences of the Christian life. But to many persons in our time it means what we do with trading stamps at a redemption center. Shall we eliminate this great word from our Christian vocabulary? Surrender it to the marketplace? Not at all! It is the responsibility of the clergy to pour relevant meaning into the word and of the laity to open themselves to that meaning.

And what shall I say of the word *love*? It surely is a term more widely used in our civilization than almost any other significant word—and not least often in church. Preachers may refer to it as a magic feeling which will solve every human problem; but the businessman being pushed by his competitor must wonder what love means, as do the two young people feeling the pressures of powerful urges and teased by the seductions of our society. Just imagine what happens in a congregation of two hundred and thirty-three people when the minister says, "Love one another." In fact, the preacher may sound angry when he says it or bark the words like a stern command, and this only adds to the confusion. So ministers must be sensitive to what they say and how they say it and the many ways in which it may be heard. Members of the congregation must be equally sensitive to what words mean in different situations and what meaning is appropriate to their own life.

• It is the barriers within ourselves which probably constitute the most serious impediment to effective communication through preaching. If we know what they are and learn how to handle them (we probably cannot remove them all), we will surely improve our skills in preaching and hearing sermons.

The *feelings* that we carry within us as we come to church may be barriers to communication. Our anxieties, fears, hostilities, prejudices—we all have an assortment of such feelings and we bring them to church. They affect the way we preach and the way we listen. It is easy for us to be defensive in church: quick to bristle at something the preacher says or quick to say something we know will make the people bristle. Tensions in our families and in our congregational life may give a peculiar tone to what we say or what we hear.

Some of the feelings may be real but not very serious. Members of one family, who attended church faithfully, once said to me, "By the time we get to church, we need it!"

The worry and hurry of getting the whole family to church on time resulted in strangely mixed feelings of frustration and anticipation. Ministers ought to be sensitive to such circumstances. And the families themselves can learn to grin and bear it.

Other feelings are more profound, more powerful, and may be more damaging. On a Sunday morning, we had sung the hymn, "This Is My Father's World." After church a member of the congregation said to me, "Chet, I can't sing that hymn. I hated my father, and he hated me!"

It is obvious that how we deliver and listen to a sermon is bound to be influenced by all these feelings boiling within us. Yet the presence of such barriers does not discredit the sermon itself. Actually, these emotions and our desire to manage them effectively constitute one of the reasons we are in church. Bringing the resources of the gospel to bear on this aspect of our personal life is one reason for sermons.

Ambivalence is a deep feeling which many of us experience as we come to church. This is Reuel Howe's wise insight. In his model, he indicates the fundamental importance of the feeling of ambivalence by putting it at the base of all the other barriers. (I have copied this in my model.)

As we come to the preaching event, we want to proclaim and hear the gospel, and yet we are also reluctant to do so. Members of the congregation know that the gospel may have some painful as well as promising things to say to us. We want to hear them but shrink from them. Preachers know this too; we stand under the same possibility of judgment. So we experience the same ambivalence in preaching the gospel that the congregation experiences in hearing it.

What Howe says so helpfully about this strange feeling has driven me to a still deeper question. Is there a barrier implicit in the gospel itself? Does our feeling of ambivalence reflect something disturbing in the gospel? I believe that there is indeed an aspect of the gospel which offends us and constitutes an unavoidable barrier to its communication.

Offense is the word used to identify this characteristic of the gospel. Paul uses the term to indicate that the gospel, for all its promise, is not easily accepted. The good news which Paul preached was offensive to some of his hearers, because it conflicted with their most deeply cherished beliefs; and to others because it unsettled their self-confidence (cf. I Cor. 1:23; Gal. 5:11). If the gospel was presented honestly, such a tension was unavoidable. Hearers had to be choosers. Paul was giving a name to what Jesus had experienced, indeed, what every genuine prophet has learned. The teachings of Jesus were offensive to some who heard him; so they rejected his message. Even the disciples who were loyal did not always understand and were sometimes uneasy about what they heard.

The offense is still part of the gospel. There is something in it which draws us to it but something which feels like a vague threat also. The affirmation that God cares about us is winsome. But the assertion that we are in such trouble that we cannot manage our lives without his help sounds like an insult. The message that we cannot earn God's favor, that he gives it to us in spite of our not deserving it, is hard for us to accept.

Shall we trim the gospel so that it fits with our own notions of what is acceptable? Or shall we recognize that the gospel is likely to be troublesome for every one of us? If we admit the latter, we have admitted that the communication of the gospel is hazardous, not just because of the methods involved, but because of some accent in the message itself and our tendency to react negatively to it. Preaching and hearing the gospel is risky business.

Let me add two notes to this discussion of the offense of the gospel.

First, as a wise friend said to me on several occasions, the gospel may well carry an implicit offense, but let's make sure the offense is in the right place. That is, let us try to speak and relate to one another so that our speech or our manner is not offensive. Let the offense be in the gospel, not in our attitudes or expressions.

This has often troubled me as a preacher. I fear that some people may reject the gospel, because they dislike something about me. All I can do is try to keep myself out of the way or let myself be a useful channel, and hope that the gospel will carry its own conviction. As a hearer, I must take the same care not to be offended by the person but to be confronted by the gospel.

Second, the attractiveness of the gospel is not simply a matter of good salesmanship. People sometimes speak about the Christian faith as if it were a product to be sold. All we have to do, they say, is to package the gospel attractively and the public will buy it. The claim is that the gospel would be more acceptable if we were better salespeople.

It is certainly wise to improve our methods and sharpen our skills for presenting the gospel. But if what I have said here is at all true, more is involved than good salesmanship. We are dealing with some of the most troublesome and tender feelings in our experience. We are caught up in some of the most significant relationships of our lives. They must be handled with care. And if the gospel really does carry a subtle offense, our most careful and caring efforts at communication may not be successful. Really listening to the gospel is risky. Not everyone is willing to take that risk.

AND WHAT OF THE HOLY SPIRIT?

At this point, someone will ask, "What does God have to do with all this?" Preachers usually raise the question, "Isn't the Holy Spirit active in the preaching event? You are reducing the sermon to an entirely human activity and leaving the Spirit out of it. Isn't God doing something too?"

My answer is not to deny that God works in the event of preaching, but to suggest that these human channels are the instrument that he must use. It would be presumptuous to say that God cannot break through to us in spite of the barriers we put in his way. But it seems reasonable to believe that the process we are studying is the means he is most likely to use. Therefore, the more we understand the process, and the more skillfully we use it, the more effectively God will be able to reach us. Barriers which interfere with our communicating with one another will also hinder his communicating with us. By reducing these interferences and opening the channels, we make it possible for him to address us more clearly. Our purpose is to present ourselves as instruments and the sermon as an occasion for the Spirit's use.

8
Preaching as Communication

What may we expect of preaching as a means of communication? In the light of what we know about the process, what may we hope to happen when we gather together for the preaching/hearing of a sermon? These are the questions to which we now turn. We will seriously consider some of the more frequent criticisms of preaching and respond in terms of our understanding of both communication and worship. Before settling to this task, however, there are two preliminary considerations I should like to offer; one relates to the occasion on which preaching occurs and the other to the participants in the event.

• The fact that people do come to church is important in our evaluation of preaching. As we have said, the communicative event is not just the sermon but the total experience of worship. The presence of people in a sanctuary, engaging in the experience of worship, surely indicates something about the potential importance of the occasion.

It would be wrong to say that because people are in church the sermon is bound to be significant, no matter what the preacher does. But it would also be unfair to say that their being there makes no difference at all in the possible effect of the sermon. A sanctuary is not a lecture hall; a sermon is not a lecture. People come to church for a variety of reasons, to be sure, but among their reasons is a sense that worship might be important.

People do not have to come to church, they choose to. They come with expectations, hopes, and concerns. This decisive quality of their presence and these attitudes give a significant dimension to the occasion for preaching. It cannot guarantee that anything important will happen, but it certainly creates a possibility, perhaps a likelihood, that something significant may be communicated.

I am aware of all the limiting factors in the occasion. Motives for being there may be mixed. It may be true that fewer come today than attended in previous decades. And what about those who are not present? (That really is a separate problem, requiring separate treatment.) All that needs to be said at this point is simply that the presence of a congregation, gathered in a sanctuary for the purpose of worship, constitutes an eloquent factor in the communicative event of preaching. Significant possibilities are present. It is up to us to take advantage of them.

• A second observation is basic to everything we shall say about preaching as a means of communication. The effectiveness of the event depends on what happens at both ends of the process. We have long understood that the way a sermon is prepared and delivered is an essential factor in its effectiveness. It is now clear, on the basis of what we know about communication, that how the listeners prepare themselves and how they receive the sermon are also important. This theme will recur again and again as we look at the several facets of communication and relate them to preaching.

Preaching and Information

One criticism of preaching is that we can hear a sermon and come away without really knowing what the preacher said. This observation is buttressed by studies which indicate that speaking-and-listening is not the most effective way of teaching and learning. It is suggested that we retain only a modest percentage of what we hear, and that this puts serious limitations on preaching.

These observations are doubtless valid. We must be realistic in our expectations of what sermons can accomplish. There is no virtue in expecting a sermon to do something it cannot do. But when we understand what is possible, we can do our best to enable these possibilities to be realized.

There may be many reasons why we leave church without any clear sense of what the preacher said. One is that the preachers themselves may not have been sure what they wanted to say. Some sermons I hear convince me that the preacher has not clearly defined the purpose and theme. This is said, not to be unkind, but to be helpful. Effective communication requires a clearly held purpose. And this, in turn, requires the careful work of the preacher.

It may also be that we listeners have not paid attention to what was said. (This may reflect on the quality of the sermon too, but more about that at another time.) The simple fact is that no form of communication will work unless we give it our attention. We can sit in a conversation and not really hear what is being said. We can listen to music on the radio and not know what is being played. We can watch a TV commercial and not really know what product or institution is being advertised. We can sit in church and not listen to the sermon.

Some months ago there was a very clever TV commercial

on one of our local stations. I enjoyed it, but I never could remember the name of the bank which was being advertised. This probably is not an unusual experience. So it is not just lectures or sermons that fail to communicate. The cleverest, most carefully contrived efforts at communication will fail unless we give them our attention.

Moral: Effective sermons require serious intention on the part of the preacher and careful attention on the part of the hearer.

Another factor is a very simple observation: Different sermons have different purposes. In order to determine whether a particular sermon succeeds in communicating, we have to ask what its purpose is. If it is said that some sermons do not convey much information, one obvious answer is that many sermons do not intend to; their purpose is quite different. Teaching is certainly one aspect of preaching. Sermons with this purpose should be carefully constructed so as to achieve maximum (even though limited) success. But not all sermons aim to teach or to give information, and such sermons must be evaluated according to their own purposes.

It may be, for instance, that all a minister wants to communicate at a given time is his excitement about some aspect of Christian faith or his discovery of some important resource for Christian living. Further details of the truth or facets of the experience can be interpreted on other occasions, in other sermons or in study groups. For the moment, the preacher may be content simply to say, "Here is something which I believe to be exciting and important for us all." And if, on this occasion, some members of the congregation catch his excitement, see his commitment, that may be enough for one day. We can engage together in further, deeper inquiry at other times.

One Sunday some years ago, as our family was gathering for dinner after church, our teenage son came running in with a mischievous grin on his face. He had just come out of the church behind two women who were discussing the morning service. He heard one say to the other, referring to my sermon, "I don't know what he said, but doesn't he say it beautifully."

I confess to mixed feelings about that comment, mostly a good-natured acceptance, without severe disappointment. I hope that they understood something of what had been said. But if they caught a sense that we were grappling with an issue of ultimate importance, that may have been enough for one Sunday morning. There would be other Sundays and other sermons; there would be other meetings with other methods.

It may not really matter either if different people seem to receive different messages from the same sermon. Most of us know that this is likely, and most sermons, in fact, allow for it to happen. But is it only sermons for which this is true? While writing this particular section, I have read two reviews of a current movie. The two reactions are strikingly different, even contradictory. Shall we conclude that movies are a poor means of communication, or shall we acknowledge that any creative medium admits of varying interpretation?

One medium may carry several messages and at several levels of meaning. That may be the genius of creative communication. Frankly, I find it neither surprising nor dismaying that people come out of church with different reactions to what has happened in the sanctuary. Why should we expect uniform response to a sermon, when we do not expect it of any other creative expression? Unanimous agreement after church might even be an indication that the sermon had failed.

Some time ago, a few churches in our city engaged in an experiment using feedback. Members of the congregations gathered after the services to discuss the sermon. Some were surprised at how many different reactions there were. They had heard the same sermon but had extracted meanings appropriate to their own needs and conditions. They were astonished and a little dismayed at the discovery. But need we be? Why not just realize that this is the way sermons communicate, and this is the way congregations receive messages.

Some sermons are designed to teach, some to convey information. Such intentions must be deliberately implemented, and such sermons thoughtfully received. Other sermons serve to communicate feeling, commitment, excitement; they point beyond a specific content and invite us to look for a further truth or experience. Such sermons cannot be measured in terms of information or even teaching effectiveness. We must wait and see whether they have touched persons at the deeper levels of motivation and meaning.

Preaching and Persuasion

How are we touched at these deeper levels? What is there about a message that moves us to take some affirmative action? These questions raise the issue of persuasion, which is another interesting area of study in communication theory.

Let's imagine a typical preaching situation. Let me be the preacher and you a member of the congregation. Let's imagine that I am communicating with reasonable effectiveness, so that you are getting the message.

At this point there are two options open to you. You can say, "You speak to my condition; I'm with you." Or you can say, "I just don't agree with what you say. I can't accept it."

What makes the difference in your response? Why are you persuaded in the one instance and not in the other? Is it simply a matter of communication? I think not.

There is a difference between communication and persuasion. [1] We must keep this distinction clear. In our imagined preaching situation, I may be communicating well enough, but you may not be persuaded to agree with the message. And the reason is not that I have failed to communicate, but that you have chosen not to be persuaded. Failure to persuade does not mean failure to communicate.

Persuasion is a deeper process than communication. It requires not only that I communicate persuasively, but that you let yourself be persuaded.

Interestingly enough, it is easier to identify factors which inhibit persuasion than it is to identify qualities that make a speaker or a message persuasive. Studies in this aspect of communication theory have discovered several attitudes and personal characteristics which make us resistant to persuasion. A summary way of stating the matter is this: The depth and certainty of our commitment to particular attitudes, values, and beliefs determine our openness to persuasion. If these beliefs lie close to the heart of our personal life, we will resist any attempt to persuade us to alter them, but we will respond warmly to any communication which reinforces them. The more intense our feelings about certain values, the less likely we are to be persuaded to modify our commitment. If what is being communicated conflicts with or challenges our deeply held, deeply felt attitudes or beliefs, we will resist the message no matter how persuasively it is presented. And this resistance is not necessarily stubbornness or bias; it may be a mark of personal integrity.

Now note this: It is precisely such profound personal commitments, deeply cherished and charged with emotion, with which significant preaching is concerned. In church we are involved with matters of ultimate importance. We are dealing not only with the meaning of our present life but with our eternal destiny. Sermons of any real merit are addressed to these matters.

Let me say it in a slightly different way. A sermon may be quite effective as communication, without being persuasive. The message may be entirely clear; it may even carry the intense feeling of the sender; but the receiver always has the option of being persuaded or not. This is an essential part of being human; it is a basic freedom which must be affirmed. And it is a necessary part of the process of communication and persuasion.

Paul's direct address to King Agrippa must have been powerful. But the king could bring himself to say only, "Almost thou persuadest me" (Acts 26:28, KJV). This has been a recurring response to the preacher from the New Testament to now.

Paul Tillich has stated the issue with directness and clarity.

> The question *cannot* be: How do we communicate the Gospel so that others will accept it? For this there is no method. To communicate the Gospel means putting it before the people so that they are able to decide for or against it. The Christian Gospel is a matter of decision. It is to be accepted or rejected. All that we who communicate this Gospel can do is to make possible a genuine decision . . . True communication of the Gospel means making a definite decision for or against it. [2]

The question remains then. What *does* persuade? If Tillich's judgment is correct, nothing guarantees persuasion. But surely some things contribute to it. In this regard, there are two aspects of communication through preaching which we will now consider.

THE CUMULATIVE EFFECT OF PREACHING

One characteristic of preaching which deserves more recognition than is commonly given is what may be called its *cumulative effect.* Criticism of preaching is sometimes based on congregational response to a single occasion. In some studies, people attending church have been given a questionnaire about the sermon. Their responses have varied. From the same sermon, different people have received different messages, and some none at all. So it is concluded that preaching is a poor method of communication.

Such a conclusion entirely overlooks the cumulative effect

of preaching. On the one hand, as we have noted, any single sermon may in fact communicate several facets of several messages. But what is even more important, no single sermon has to do the whole job. There is always next Sunday and the next and the next. Wise ministers know very well that on any given occasion, some messages get through to some people, others get through to others, and some do not get through at all. So they return to the central issues again and again. Important themes recur, and what does not get through this time may get through next time, maybe next year.

Our son once said to me, "Dad, you're always saying the same thing."

My reply was, "Yeah, I only have one thing to say." And that is profoundly true. The thrust of my preaching was to affirm and affirm again, in as many ways as I knew how, what I believed to be the central claims of Christian faith, the deepest resources of Christian experience. In a sense, it added up to "the same thing."

Writers on persuasion recognize that persuasion takes time. One single effort will not accomplish the desired result. Advertisers certainly know this; they set up campaigns. Surely, we as preachers and hearers of sermons ought to know it as well. Preaching is a recurring occasion. We open ourselves to its possibilities by returning to worship as regularly as we can.

Let me report part of a conversation with a man in the last community I served. He was a member of another denomination, president of a college, theologically trained, a respected leader in the community. He shared with me a conversation he had with a member of our congregation.

The friend asked our member, "How's Pennington doing over at Hennepin?"

Our member replied, "He's trying to preach grace. And it ain't easy."

The man who shared the exchange with me considered this a very significant response. I agreed.

Our member was a devout Christian man, respected in the community. He was also a warm supporter of my ministry. He had been nurtured on an earlier understanding of Christianity in which not much was said about grace. He had learned that being a Christian means being a person of strong moral character and a responsible participant in the community. Now in my preaching he was hearing a different accent which, without questioning the integrity of his belief and practice, was challenging him to a different understanding of himself and his relation to God.

No wonder he said, "It ain't easy."

But the grace being proclaimed was not limited to a single or even an occasional sermon. There were personal conversations and study groups. There were business meetings. Central to it all was his regular attendance at church and sermons in which he heard "the same thing." Grace was operative, however articulated or understood.

This man, by the way, would be the first to testify to the importance of preaching in his own Christian development. He would not attribute his growth to just his current preacher, but the one before that, and before that, back to the quiet beginnings of Christian experience.

Many laypersons would bear a similar witness to the significance of preaching in their personal Christian experience. Indeed, many clergy would testify that an important element in their vocational decision was the influence of preachers whom they knew and respected. Such testimony ought not be forgotten or denied because of occasional or fragmentary surveys. We can recognize the cumulative effect of preaching and be thankful. If God does not reach us on one occasion, he will try again.

THE CONTEXT OF PREACHING

There is another aspect of preaching which must be mentioned, even though briefly: The context of the sermon is an important factor in its persuasiveness. We recognize that preaching does not take place in isolation from other actions and events. The channel of communication, we have said, is the whole service of worship. The sights and symbols of the sanctuary "speak". Hymns and prayers are not just "preliminaries" to the sermon; they are integral parts of the communication process. If "nothing never communicates," then everything that happens is saying something. The liturgy may speak to someone who may receive little from the sermon, or liturgy and sermon may reinforce one another in communicating the gospel.

Then there is the wider context of the minister's total life with the congregation. Study groups examine the message heard from the pulpit. Small groups mediate the grace proclaimed in sermons. The pastor's ministry in times of crisis and the members' care for one another express the love affirmed in preaching. Pastor and people work together to implement in congregation and community the concerns which are voiced in sermons.

Obviously, much more could be said about this aspect of preaching. It is enough now simply to affirm the wholeness of ministry and the importance of the entire web of relationships between minister and congregation and among the members themselves. The persuasive influence of sermons fits together with the cumulative effects of our life and work together as a congregation.

Preaching and Credibility

The discussion of persuasion leads easily to the question of credibility. What is it that makes a speaker credible? Again studies in communication theory are helpful to us. Considerable work has been done in what is called *source credibility*. The central question is: What are the characteristics of sources or senders (preachers) which cause them to be accepted as credible by the receivers (congregation)?

At first glance, the burden of credibility seems to fall on the sender. The empirical studies of the subject affirm an ethical conclusion: *Credibility is, in the final analysis, a moral quality of the sender.* For our purposes, this means that when ministers enter the pulpit and advocate certain truths about God or the meaning of life, we expect some consistency between what they say and who they are.

Before the laity relaxes, however, we must note a further conclusion reached by these studies: *The credibility of the sender must be accepted and affirmed by the receiver.* One of the most careful students of the subject offers the following observation: "The amount of credibility that an individual is seen to have is a function of who the receiver is, what the topic is, and what the interpretation is. [It] depends on the relationship between the source and the receiver."[3] In other words, the preacher's credibility is in the minds and hearts of the congregation. This puts a corresponding burden on the laity as they form judgments about clergy. Preachers must seek to be genuine. The congregation must seek to be honest. Whether people receive the preacher as credible is their own private judgment.

The question of credibility looks two ways. (1) Preacher, are you really what you want the people to think you are? (2) Church member, are you honest and informed in your feeling toward and your evaluation of your minister?

Careful analyses of the process of persuasion have identified three elements which, taken together, contribute to the credibility of the sender: *competence, trustworthiness,* and *dynamism.* There are some differences of vocabulary among the studies, but these terms are representative and accurately reflect the conclusions. The relevance of these qualities applied to the preaching and hearing of sermons will be apparent.

Competence is clearly a matter of training and experience. The claim to competence for oneself and the acknowledgment of competence in another is a sensitive matter. In exactly what areas may a preacher claim competence? That depends on training and experience. Clergy might wisely be modest at this point. Neither education nor ordination confers wisdom in all matters, and stepping into a pulpit does not automatically confer authority.

By the same token, in what areas are laity willing to accept the competence of clergy? On the basis of a few decades of experience, I can testify that laity does not easily yield authority to clergy, even in areas in which the clergy may be expected to have some competence.

The obvious moral to be drawn might well be: Let clergy and laity togoether commit themselves to gaining competence in matters about which the church is primarily concerned. (That ought to be material for several sermons and many study groups.)

The second attribute of credibility is *trustworthiness*. It is closely related to competence, because we are likely to trust only those who have demonstrated some skill in their field. But trustworthiness is a moral quality which goes somewhat deeper than competence. It implies being also honest and genuine. It means that the speaker is personally committed to whatever is being advocated for the receiver.

So we ask serious questions about preachers. Do they really mean what they are saying? Can we trust their integrity? But in asking such searching questions of others, we must address them to ourselves. Do we understand our own reaction to the preacher? Do we know what is going on inside ourselves? Can we trust our own judgment?

These are difficult and awkward questions. It is easier to address them to others, but honesty requires that we look within ourselves as well. We must be able to trust our own evaluations of the trustworthiness of others.

The third characteristic of credibility is *dynamism*. A variety of descriptive adjectives is used by different investigators to identify this quality: aggressive, emphatic, forceful, energetic.[4] In a word, a credible speaker must be dynamic.

One churchman said to me, "So many preachers I hear

sound bored. I don't know whether it's their technique or their attitude. But they sound bored." This man was not being mean or vindictive. He loves the church and wants preachers to be effective. He regretted having to say what he did.

Obviously, if a preacher *sounds* bored, the congregation will *be* bored. The preacher will certainly not be regarded as credible, and the message will surely not be persuasive. Credibility requires a certain intensity of manner, a forcefulness in presentation.

Personally, I see dynamism as being rooted in conviction and commitment. Dorothy Sayers (I think it was she) commented that it is a sin to make the gospel dull and uninteresting. I would venture to say that, if preachers are really convinced of the truth of the gospel and seized by its power, there will be an intensity in their manner of preaching, even if a quiet intensity, which will convey credibility. If we are deeply committed to the Lord in whose name we minister, there will surely be an enthusiasm and energy which will be communicated in our message.

I remember one preacher very well. He was tall, husky, good-humored, and intense about his faith. As a teenager, I sat with the youth choir behind the pulpit from which this man preached. I can almost see his body now: hands gripped tightly behind his back, fingers clasping and unclasping nervously, body stretched up on tiptoe, swaying over the pulpit, strong shoulders adding their thrust to the forcefulness of his voice. Talk about dynamism! He had it. And I could not help but be persuaded that he really meant what he was saying; he wanted us to believe with him and to enjoy the benefits of a faith he found so compelling.

Does this mean that every effective preacher must have charisma? Hardly. We are what we are. And most of us are not so fortunate as to be blessed with charisma. What is required, I suspect, is that our personal powers be liberated, so that they may be freely used in communicating the gospel.

This is not easily achieved and may be blocked by all sorts of personal characteristics which have nothing to do with our integrity. As clergy, however, we may well pray for the grace of dynamism, which will allow the gospel to be persuasively communicated through our preaching.

And what shall we who are hearers pray for? Competence and trustworthiness, we have said. We hardly need dynamism in order to hear the gospel. What we need is openness to receive and honesty to commit ourselves to its claims.

But then we who are receivers become, in turn, senders. It is imperative that we laypersons realize that we are the preachers to those outside the church.[5] So our competence and trustworthiness become doubly significant, not only that we may receive the gospel "into honest and good hearts," but that we may be able to restate it in our daily conversations with our friends and associates. At this point, our special dynamism as laypersons may be very important. We may not need the forceful qualities of a public speaker, except as that becomes our opportunity; but we surely need the quiet dynamism of persons who are deeply and truly committed to the One whose message we bear.

Preaching and Listening

Feedback is at once a scientific term with specialized technical meaning and a household word with all sorts of informal popular uses. In the study of communication, feedback designates a very important part of the process.

When we try to communicate with other persons, we hope they will get the message just as we have sent it. But how can we know this? The act of decoding and receiving takes place within the receiver. We can know what is actually happening only as the receiver feeds back signals which will indicate what meaning has been received and in what manner. These signals may be nonverbal: frowns of annoyance or disagreement, smiles of appreciation. Or they may be verbal: questions for clarification or a restatement of the message as received. Senders who really care about the message will solicit such feedback.

In our terms, feedback is the congregation's response to the sermon. Church members reflect back to the preacher what they have heard, what they understood the preacher to be saying. The preacher, then, becomes listener. This is an essential part of effective communication in the church.

There are two values in this process. First of all, communication is tested by feedback. Preachers know what they intended to say. The question is what did the congregation actually hear. We have seen how complex the process is. The possibilities of interference or distortion are enormous. The only way we can know how well the process is working, how clearly the message is being transmitted, is to test by feedback.

Furthermore, communication is improved by feedback. Meanings are clarified and deepened when we talk with one another about the message. Studies have demonstrated quite impressively that feedback greatly improves the effectiveness of communication. To jump to the conclusion that there can be no useful communication without feedback is to go beyond the evidence of these studies and to deny the evidence of our experience. But we would be wise to acknowledge the clear value of feedback in improving the effectiveness of preaching-and-hearing sermons.

And now, language being what it is, there is *feedforward.* This is the process in which response is solicited and given while the message is still being designed; and that input adds to the shape and content of the message in its final form. Some ministers have developed this practice in sermon seminars, engaging the laity in the preparation of the sermon.[6]

The effectiveness of feedback or feedforward depends on the willingness to listen as well as to speak, at both ends of the process. Clergy, usually regarded as the talkers, must be open to hearing the laity. Laity, usually regarded as the listeners, must be willing to speak openly.

Let me comment first to the clergy. We clergy do not always listen—really listen—to the laity. This is somewhat odd, since we are trained to listen in counseling, but it seems difficult to transfer that skill to the preaching situation. There may be many reasons for this: our sense that in this realm we are the experts or our defensiveness about preaching. The fact remains that, if we are to be effective communicators, we must be good listeners, really hearing what our members are saying, knowing what they are feeling and thinking.

And laypeople: Are we really willing to hear what the preachers are saying? And do we respond with honesty and thoughtfulness? Many preachers are troubled about what they see happening in our civilization. They are genuinely concerned about our well-being. They want to share Christian resources with us. They may even be anxious about our eternal destiny. Can we really hear all that?

Then can we, as Christian persons, respond with honest and thoughtful reflection? It is not very useful just to say, "I enjoyed your sermon," or even to say, "I didn't like it at all." Surely, we can engage in more significant communication about matters of profound importance.

This may challenge us, both lay and clergy. It may force us to increase our competence, so that we know what we are talking about. It will certainly improve our communication with one another and—dare we say—with God.

This kind of two-way communication will go beyond the Sunday service. It will require participation in other kinds of activity. There may be sermon seminars to help plan the message or feedback sessions to share what we heard. Groups will meet for study and discussion. Family conversations may take on deeper dimensions.

As we open ourselves to one another, we are opening ourselves to God. His word will be addressed to us in many ways. Preachers will hear the word, not only in their study and preparation, but in their conversations with their members and their contacts in the community. Church members will hear the word, not only in sermons, but in conversations about sermons and in continuing study of the issues involved. By engaging together in what is prosaically called feedback, we are allowing the Holy Spirit to reach us in many different ways; we are enabling God to communicate with us more effectively.

Transition: From Communication . . .

So that's what communication is all about. It's a miracle that it ever happens at all! To enable it to happen obviously demands the wise use of the best gifts we can bring to the occasion.

This is why I believe that *effective communication is a creative task*. The process, as we have seen, is dismayingly complex. The barriers are unbelievably awkward. The limitations in both sender and receiver are subtle but inhibiting. It takes a lot of skill to get the message through.

The message! We really have not said much about that. Yet one purpose of communication (certainly of preaching) is to transmit a message. We have studied the process and looked at the persons involved in communication. Now we must turn to the consideration of another important element in communication—the message and its delivery. This is also a significant part of studies in persuasion.[7]

There is evidence that an important factor in persuasive communication is the shape of the message. A message must be designed to communicate what the sender intends to say, to make its way through the barriers in the process, and to be received with a minimum of distortion. How do we design a message so that it communicates? That is a creative task. How do we present a message so that it gets across? That is a creative task. How do we receive a message so as not to distort it, but to hear it truly? That too is a creative task.

We turn now from the study of communication to the study of creativity. . . .

PART 3

PREACHING AS CREATIVE EVENT

Transition, Continued: . . . to Creativity

. . . We turn to the study of creativity, because *effective communication is a creative task*. The gifts required for persuasive communication are the gifts of creative expression.

• Shaping a message so that it communicates with clarity and persuasiveness is a creative task. A sermon is a work of art designed to convey a meaning. Such a work is not put together casually. It is carefully constructed with a view to accomplishing its purpose. This surely calls for craftsmanship and creative labor.

• Delivering a message so that it makes its way through all the barriers of the communication process is a creative task. How shall it be presented so as to express its meaning with a minimum of static or interference in the process? How shall it be delivered so as to carry with it the urgency and commitment of the sender? If the message is to be persuasive, the sender (preacher) must deliver oneself with the message. How does one do this? It is a creative achievement.

• Receiving a message is also a task requiring imagination and sensitivity, which are creative gifts. To receive a message without distorting it requires an imaginative participation with the sender in the event of communication. To hear a sermon honestly calls for an openness, a willingness to receive, which is not just a passive quality but a creative attitude.

What, then, is creativity? How do we engage in a creative task? What may we do to enter into a creative event? These are the questions to which we now turn.

As I see it, there are two arts that a preacher must master in order to communicate effectively. The first is the art of writing. A preacher must know how to put a sermon together so that it will accomplish its purpose. The work of preparing a sermon is a task of creative design. Then, second, the message which has been carefully created must be effectively delivered. For this the preacher must exercise the art of public speech or dramatic delivery. In preaching a sermon, a preacher refashions with the congregation what has been shaped in the study. This is an art.

And what shall we say of the creative work of the congregation? We will reflect on this as we look at the minister's creative tasks, trying to determine how the congregation can participate in them. Effective hearing is an important dimension of effective preaching.

One final introductory word . . .

To the laity: Effective preaching requires your appreciation and support of the creative dimensions of the minister's tasks.

To the clergy: Intentionally creative labor will give you your deepest fulfillment as a person and as a minister.

To you both: This is where the joy is.

9
The Meaning of Creativity

I wish we could join in a celebration of the mystery and miracle of human creativity. We take it so much for granted, yet it is one of the most significant aspects of our humanity. There is no way to measure the beauties and joys which come into our lives through the exercise and appreciation of our creative gifts: whether it be the pictures we put on the walls of our rooms, the music so immediately accessible to us, the meals we enjoy, the inventions which make life easier, the flowers we plant in the yard, or the view from our window.

How does it happen that we human beings have the capacity to make something (a piece of sculpture, a poem, a cake) and also the capacity to respond to what someone else makes (the word of appreciation, the burst of applause, the look of wonder)? This is surely one of the special gifts with which we are blessed.

Our creativity takes many forms, which we cannot possibly catalog without missing someone's favorite. I can only cite some which are most obvious to me: an artist before a canvas, a potter bent over a mound of clay, a sculptor wresting shapes from stone or steel, a scientist or a team of scientists patiently examining a problem, an inventor putting things together again and again until they work, an executive making lonely decisions, a teacher agonizing over a student's destiny, persons imagining themselves in each other's place, parents spending their energies on chosen priorities—and, yes, a preacher standing with the congregation, pouring disciplined gifts and personal graces into the communication of shared truths.

The creative occasion which really impresses me most profoundly is a public performance, perhaps of music or drama. Here at least three mysteries come together in a uniquely human experience.

There is, first, the mystery of the writer or composer who has arranged words or sounds, or both, in such a way as to convey a message to be shared with others—a story, a relationship, a vision.

There is the mystery of the performing artist, who enacts the words, the sounds, so as to re-create the message, the meaning, and communicate it to the audience.

There is the mystery of us in the audience, who have the capacity to receive the meaning, to respond to the artistry, and to experience in ourselves what both the author and the performer intend us to experience. In the presence of these mysteries, an entire audience can be hushed in awe, moved to tears, shouting in excitement, or exploding into laughter.

This is a miracle. What is there about us that makes it possible? What makes it possible for a person to create works which will touch and move and delight other persons? And what makes it possible for us to respond to such works, to be touched and moved and delighted as both maker and performer intended? How does it happen?

That's the way the question was put to Mrs. Pennington and me one night by a perceptive friend. We were returning from a symphony concert which had been very exciting. As we shared our appreciation of what we had experienced, our friend asked, "How did music ever happen? It's so unnecessary."

We knew what she meant. The enjoyment of beauty seems a sheer bonus. We do not need it as we need food, clothing, and shelter. But perhaps more profoundly we do need it. We humans do not live by bread alone but by beauty as well. We have gifts of expression by which we are fulfilled and gifts of enjoyment by which our lives are enriched.

How does it happen?

A Universal Gift

This fact of human creativity has fascinated me for years. I have sensed the wonder and beauty of it all and have believed that it has profound relevance to the preaching and hearing of sermons. So the opportunity to inquire more deeply into the mystery of creativity and its workings has brought me both delight and discovery.

Over the past twenty-five years there has been extensive research into this human capacity. As in the study of communication, there are varieties of approach and interpretation, and we may learn from them all. Reading about creativity and sharing the reflections of creative artists has deepened my wonder at and appreciation for this extraordinary human gift.

Interestingly enough, these studies indicate that it is difficult, probably impossible, to define creativity. There is much that eludes measurement, which can only be observed, described, and interpreted. Rollo May offers a simple definition of the creative process, as "the process of *bringing something new into being*" (italics his).[1] The gift of creativity, then, is the capacity to make something. Many creative persons prefer to speak of themselves simply as makers. To create is to make. This would seem to apply to anything: a poem, a song, a novel, a cake, a decision, a machine, a sermon.

Not only is it difficult to say exactly what creativity is, it is equally difficult to know how this gift is related to other aspects of personality. One study of creative scientists suggests that intelligence may be related to creativity, although the connection is not at all clear. But the same study also speaks of motivation and persistence as important elements in creative achievement.[2] So we must ask what determines motivation and persistence. The answer to this may be more important than the measurement of intelligence and more mysterious. Between two persons of apparently equal talent, what motivates one to work more persistently than the other?

I have often wondered about the relationship between *natural gift* and *acquired skill.* In discussions with artists and teachers of artists, I have received no satisfactory interpretation. Obviously, some people are more gifted than others, in terms of both talent and intelligence, but this is not the same as being more creative. What makes the difference? It is hard, if not impossible, to say. In fact, one study of leading artists and scientists claims to have found "only one trait that stood out in common among individuals. This was a willingness to work hard and to work long hours."[3] If that observation seems mundane and ordinary, we shall have occasion to note its importance.

There is one significant agreement among students of creativity, namely, that *every person has the fundamental capacity for creative achievement and appreciation.* There may be great differences in talent and intelligence, but regardless of these, we all have the basic gift of creativity. We all can be creative, do creative things, enjoy creative experiences. As one author puts it, "Every man has energies which he can develop into creative work."[4]

A recent study, entitled quite simply *The Creative*

Experience, consists of interviews with twenty-three persons who are recognized as having made outstanding contributions in the arts and sciences. Most of these persons express their conviction that "everyone is creative to some degree and that the creative experience is not reserved for a few.' [5]

Creativity is a universal gift. We may possess it in varying degrees, but we share the common gift. We need not be a star or a genius or an outstanding leader in order to be creative. We may be quite anonymous persons, but we can be creative in the way we make whatever we have to make (whether poems or music or meals or decisions or tools or ideas). We can experience the joy of creative achievement in the way we enter into relationships with others, in the way we manage our lives.

There is evidence that we not only can but we need to experience such joys. Our creative gifts were given to us for the enrichment of our lives and the lives of others. What we do may be simple, everyday, mundane; but it may be profoundly satisfying, because it expresses our own special ability. If we stifle these powers, we are frustrated. If we misuse them, we are restless. To live well means to live creatively.

I cannot resist mentioning that this seems to be at least one meaning of Jesus' familiar parable of the talents (Matt. 25:14-29). Although the word *talent* in its biblical use means "money," its modern meaning is equally appropriate. God has given us abilities and gifts of expression. What is important is not how many we have but how we use them. Using our gifts creatively yields increased capacity for achievement ("I will set you over much") and joy ("enter into the joy of your master").

The Mark of Our Maker

This universal gift has an important religious meaning. Our creativity is a mark of our Maker. The human capacity to create is an aspect of the divine image that we bear.

The classic affirmation of Hebrew and Christian faith is that the human creature is made "in the image of God" (Gen. 1:26-27). Throughout the history of Christian thought there have been many different interpretations of this *imago dei*. Some of our ablest teachers have affirmed that it is our capacity for creative expression and appreciation which constitutes the image of God. To paraphrase a famous verse of Scripture, we make because he first made us.

Dorothy Sayers, who was as profound as she was gifted, put it quite directly, "The characteristic common to God and man is apparently that: the desire and ability to make things." [6] She quotes a beautiful statement by the famous Russian thinker Nicholas Berdyaev. "God created man in his own image and likeness, ie, made him a creator too, calling him to free spontaneous activity and not to formal obedience to His power. Free creativeness is the creature's answer to the great call of its Creator. Man's creative work is the fulfilment of the Creator's secret will." [7]

With quiet eloquence another writer speaks of the artist as "the humble servant, who with bated breath and trembling excitement recognizes in the work of his hands the image of God." [8]

My understanding of our human condition forces me to add that this mark of our origin, so indelibly engraved in our personality, is also seriously marred. The powers granted us have been misused and are now present within us in distorted forms. As a famous theologican of an earlier generation taught some of us so graphically and powerfully, our creative powers can be used destructively. This truth has important implications which go far beyond the scope of our present study. But it is certainly relevant to the question of how we release and direct these powers.

We can believe that God wills for us to find the effective expression of our creative ability. The capacity to act creatively is his gift to us. His purpose is that we use our powers for the enrichment of our life together as human beings. If we have misused this endowment, he continues to work with us to bring us to our proper fulfillment. If we have marred his image, he wills to restore it to its proper shape and meaning.

One further reflection is relevant at this point. If our creative gifts are indeed God's endowment is it not appropriate that we use these gifts in the act of worshiping him? Is it not precisely in worship and in the preaching and hearing of sermons that we ought to summon up our most distinctive endowments of imagination and creative expression?

10
The Creative Process

If we cannot define creativity, we can identify some of the personal qualities that are present in creative people. It is significant to note that there is almost universal agreement in naming two of these characteristics, discipline and receptivity. Most creative people accept the disciplines required for the effective use of their special gifts and are sensitive to everything that is happening in the creative event. Let us examine these observations and see how they may relate to our interest in preaching and hearing sermons.

The Necessity of Discipline

Creative achievement is hard work. Creativity yields joy, but it is a joy which comes by way of disciplined effort. Even when a discovery seems to come as a sudden insight or flash of inspiration, it is the fruit of concentrated toil. Even when a performance gives the appearance of ease and naturalness or a flow of words seems smooth and effortless, creative accomplishment is the result of disciplined work. To make something of value or beauty or usefulness may be a labor of love, but it is unmistakably labor.

I have already cited the observation that a common trait among creative persons is their willingness to work hard and long. Another study concludes: "It is clear that discovery and invention in both science and art require the exercise of creative imagination. And the creative process seems to be basically the same in both fields: a mind trained and attuned to possibilities, an immense amount of work and methodical planning, then leaps of intuitive insight, followed by swift consolidation." [1]

W. H. Auden reflects on the artist's task in an interesting manner. "An artist . . . should think of himself primarily as a craftsman, a 'maker,' not as an 'inspired' genius." Later Auden adds that the difference between an artist and a carpenter (who is another craftsman) is that "when the carpenter starts work he knows exactly what the finished product will be, whereas the artist never knows just what he is going to make until he has made it. But, like the carpenter, all he can or should consciously think about is how to make it as well as possible." [2]

Another author affirms that "the 'artist' bears close relation to the 'craftsman'." This implies that creative artists (the author is discussing writing) must "learn the structure of their art." An artist "must depend first of all on discipline in the simplest details as well as in the most exalted intentions of his task." So a creative artist must acquire a "habit of work." [3]

All of this seems to imply that, if we want to accomplish anything, we must simply set ourselves to the task and stay with it. A piece of work is no less creative if, instead of being caught up in an ecstasy of inspiration, we just settle down and do what is required. One composer was asked whether the creative process can be forced. He replied in the affirmative, by which he meant that sometimes we must get to work whether we feel like it or not. And in the discipline of setting our powers to the task, something creative may happen.

Releasing the Unconscious

Most creative persons are agreed that the sources of creativity are deep in the hidden regions of the self. Different writers identify this part of the personality by different terms: the subconscious, the unconscious, the preconscious. Whatever we may name it, we can certainly agree that this dimension of the self is the wellspring of creative activity.

The creative power of the subconscious mind is commonly recognized by artists and scientists. They have learned to rely upon and make use of these deep forces. One remark by a playwright is typical, "I try to let the unconscious do as much work as possible." It is reported that Ernest Hemingway told his friends that half his work was done in his subconscious mind.[4]

Some years ago I was talking with Jim Crane, an artist whom my wife and I admire both as a person and as a painter. I asked him how he paints. Does he sit down and say grimly, "I must put something on that canvas"? He replied, "By the time I start towards the canvas, something is already happening inside me." That is, the creative process starts deep within him, beyond his awareness, before he consciously decides to paint. It is this inner stirring which impels him to the canvas.

Such an understanding of ourselves is important for all of us, whether artists or not. It means that the deepest powers of our self are not only the dark and dangerous forces identified by the psychoanalyst and the therapist but are also the creative, life-affirming forces experienced by the artist and the scientist.

Jacques Maritain, in a profound analysis of human creativity, goes so far as to distinguish between two distinct regions of the unconscious. The unconscious about which Freud and his followers taught us so much, Maritain claims, is not the deepest dimension of our being. Deeper still is what he calls "the spiritual unconscious." This "preconscious of the spirit" is the seat of creative, healing, life-affirming powers. It is here that "poetry and poetic inspiration have their primal source." Here, in this "single root of the soul's powers," intuition, intellect, and imagination come together in the creative experience.[5] It is not necessary that we follow the details of Maritain's speculations. What is important is to recognize that deep within us are these dramatically mixed powers, which trouble our life but enrich it as well.

We must also know that the release of these deep forces is related to the disciplined use of our conscious powers. Every study that I have read affirms the importance of intentional effort in giving direction to the deep-moving powers which generate creative achievement.

Rollo May states this very clearly. He asserts that the insights which well up out of the unconscious come *"only in the areas to which the person is intensively committed in his conscious living."* (The italics are his.) He adds that the inspiration may come in a time of relaxation, when the problem may seem to have been set aside. But the discovery comes precisely "in those areas in which the person has worked laboriously and with dedication in his conscious experience."[6]

The creative process, then, is a sort of interactive rhythm between the conscious and the unconscious. We concentrate the best efforts of our mind upon the project at hand, whether it be resolving a problem, designing a garment, or writing a song. Then we set it aside, allowing the deeper creative powers to work on it. We may move back and forth repeatedly between these two activities. Out of the interaction will come the creative solution: the correct answer, the proper design, the right word. Then we must turn our critical attention to the solution itself, to test it, to evaluate it or to refine it.

"Open to Surprise"

Another aspect of creative experience is our attitude of openness or receptivity. Everyone who reflects on the process of creativity realizes that such an attitude is essential. Our conscious effort is accompanied by a readiness to receive anything that may happen in the experience. One psychologist calls it "an intensity of awareness." Another speaks of "openness to experience." A poet, however, is most expressive of all; we must, she says, be "open to surprise."

You probably have your own experiences of what has happened when you were "open to surprise." Let me share a modest one with you.

Recently I was asked to preach on a subject about which I had literally never preached in all my years in the parish. So I went through the usual disciplines of reading the appropriate Scripture lessons, studying what the commentaries had to say, arranging and rearranging the ideas that came to me. All this occurred over a period of several days.

The most exciting insight into the subject came to me at about 3:00 A.M., during a sleepless period. When I awoke, the idea was still with me (I had not got up to write it down—something of a risk). But midnight thoughts often look different in the light of day. So this had to be tested, examined, put in the context of the developing sermon. And it proved to be just as exciting as it had originally appeared. The text had opened me to surprise.

In reading about scientific invention or problem-solving or artistic creation, it is impressive how often the word *discovery* is used. Again and again, persons noted for their creative achievements will affirm that they did not really create anything, they simply discovered what is already there. Something came to them. From where? The answer is from the disciplined interplay of concentration and reflection, from the deep powers of the self, stimulated to action by the person's intensive effort.

One summer afternoon in Aspen, Colorado, I had a fascinating conversation with an Austrian composer. I asked him how he created a musical composition. He responded excitedly, "I don't create anything. I simply see something . . . hear something that is already there. I am not a creator, I am only a visionary. And what I see, I try to shape into a vision that others can see too." Again and again he said, "I don't create. I only discover."

Similarly, the poet writes of "the passionate patience" with which she must listen to experience and discover "the music inherent in the material." Sometimes, in her urgency to create, she tries to force the process, but this seldom succeeds. At such times she writes, "I was straining to *find words;* the word had not found *me.*" With quiet eloquence, she affirms "to write is to listen."[7]

I should like to inscribe that insight on the mind of every preacher: "To write is to listen." It has many Christian implications on which we all might profitably reflect. But we have more prosaic work to do. We must ask whether our understanding of creativity has any significance for the preaching and hearing of sermons.

Toward Creative Ministries

The preceding reflections may seem to have most relevance to the clergy, and this is probably inevitable. But in a larger sense, they are important for the laity too.

In the first place, if the theses are true, they are true for everyone, and it surely will be helpful for all of us to consider how they apply to our lives. Suggestions which are useful for the clergy may be adaptable to laity. We all will live better if we can design our habits so that our creative powers will be given a chance to work.

More directly, however, we are concerned with the

preaching and hearing of sermons. It is my conviction that, by knowing what is required for the creative ministry of the clergy, laity may enter more fully and more effectively into the life of the church. Ministers are not simply, or even primarily, business executives. They are also creative thinkers and members of a caring profession. These dimensions of ordained ministry can be supported by laity who understand what is involved; the laity, in turn, will be better served by their ministers; and we all may engage creatively in our respective ministries.

THESIS: CREATIVE WORK TAKES TIME

There is a rhythm between concentrated effort and quiet reflection. We work intently at a task, then set it aside for a while. It seems to be "out of mind"; but actually our subconscious mind, in its own creative manner, is still working on the task. Then we bring it forward for further concentrated attention. Productivity is stimulated by such a rhythm, and that takes time.

Ordinarily, the creative process cannot be rushed. There are exceptions, to be sure, and we all have experienced them. Most preachers can point to sermons which, due to emergencies, were prepared under unusual pressure, and they turned out to be rather effective sermons. Laypersons can cite similar experiences. But we must recognize that these are, in fact, exceptions. We can't have an emergency every Friday! The effective use of our creative powers requires the investment of regular periods of time.

COROLLARY: CREATIVE WORK REQUIRES BLOCKS OF TIME

We cannot hope to be really effective if we try to squeeze our creative work in between other tasks. Peter Drucker is convincing when he argues that the "knowledge worker" (and this includes the clergy) must learn to work in "fairly large chunks" of time. "Small driblets are no time at all." [8]

The concentration required for creative achievement demands consecutive, uninterrupted attention to the task at hand. For most writers, this means regular hours at the writing table. This is what the author we cited before meant by a "habit of work." We discover what our most productive hours are and devote them to our primary tasks.

COROLLARY: CREATIVE WORK DESERVES OUR BEST TIME

Whatever our creative work may be, we should turn to it while our energies are still fresh, while our minds are still uncluttered by other necessary responsibilities. It is unproductive to try to be creative when our minds are distracted by other issues and our energies already half spent on other tasks. Creative work deserves to be given our best time.

COROLLARY: OUR CREATIVE POWERS NEED NURTURE

All of us are harried by too many things to do; our time gets cluttered up with miscellaneous demands. If we are to be creative persons, we must find time to feed and nourish our deepest powers. Most of the tasks we do require the spending of creative resources. How shall they be replenished? How shall we restore the capacities we need for the many responsibilities that fill our days and half our nights?

The nurture of our creative powers requires regular times of restoration and refreshment. For the clergy, this is what I call "general study." All of us, if we are to continue to grow and develop as persons, must discover some equivalent opportunity.

CONCLUSION: WE MUST ORDER OUR LIVES SO AS TO NURTURE AND RELEASE OUR CREATIVITY

Peter Drucker argues most forcefully that the first achievement of effective leaders must be the creative ordering of their time.[9] I was uneasily amused to read his description of how difficult it is for top executives to control their time. It sounds like so much talk I hear among preachers. We all experience this to some extent. But Drucker's argument is most convincing; creative achievement requires that we organize our time so as to give our creativity opportunity to work.

COROLLARY: "ROUTINE WORK DRIVES OUT CREATIVE WORK"

This corollary is my restatement of a principle which was formulated by a university president. He had come to a new job, eagerly anticipating a creative and exciting opportunity. To his dismay, he soon found that routine responsibilities were taking up most of his time; and creative planning and dreaming, which he had hoped to accomplish, were pushed aside. So in frustrated good humor, he formulated what he called The First Law of Academic Pseudodynamics. My somewhat simplified version of his law is my endorsement: Routine work drives out creative work.[10]

This is surely relevant to everybody but perhaps in a special way to ministers. More than most persons, clergy are free to organize their own time: no clock to punch, no fixed time to report in, a variety of tasks to arrange according to one's own judgment. This is a great privilege but also a great temptation. The danger lies in the awful accuracy of the corollary stated here. Unless we establish firm and clear priorities, routine work will drive out creative work. We will be busy, but not creatively productive. Careful attention to this principle will enhance your creativity—I guarantee it.

Ministers are often uneasy about the varieties of demand to which they must respond. Actually, the many-sided shape of our ministry is really a blessing. We are privileged to enter into varieties of experience, and this can be stimulating. We can develop a rhythm among our various tasks, moving from one to another, giving each the energies and talents demanded. But effective rhythm requires design, intentional planning, established priorities. One need is constant; give creative work its proper place in the multiplicity of tasks.

However, if Drucker and the university president are right, every one of us works under such pressures. And we will be more creative if we keep routine work in its proper place (secondary, or less).

COROLLARY: STRUCTURE IS NOT RESTRICTIVE BUT RELEASING

Many of us, laity and clergy alike, resist the exhortation to organize our lives and order our priorities. We fear being caught in rigid restrictive habits. The fact is that a well-ordered pattern of work releases our creative powers, frees them for their most productive achievement.

Once we know what is of central importance in our lives, our powers can be organized around that center. Once we know what tasks have priority, other tasks take the place assigned to them. Many people are harried and fretful because they have so many things to do and no real sense of what must be done and what can be left undone. We are delivered from busyness and released into usefulness by knowing what we want most to accomplish.

A MODEL FOR MINISTERS

Now let me address the clergy directly and invite the laity to listen in. This is one of the points at which it is very important for the laity to understand some of the decisions which clergy must make. It is not that our demands are unlike those laid upon other people; they are probably quite similar. But the special nature of the ordained ministry and the special relations between clergy and congregation require special understandings. Our life and work together will be enhanced by an awareness of and sensitivity to the issues being discussed here.

If we ministers were to organize our lives according to the

theses we have just considered, what would our work schedule look like? Let me attempt a model which is obviously based on my own experience. It is simple and even unfinished, so that you may adapt it to your own way of working and your own priorities. I will refer only to the tasks which relate directly to preaching. You will see that there is plenty of time left for pastoral and administrative responsibilities. Emergencies and special needs will, of course, be given the attention they require, but we cannot put these into a schedule.

	mon	tue	wed	thu	fri	sat	sun
morning	misc	→ sermon → preparation ↘ → general study					worship sermon
afternoon							
evening							

Now let me interpret the model.

For ministers who preach on Sunday, the service of worship is the event toward which the whole week moves. Preparation for that occasion has top priority among all the tasks of the week.

In this model, Monday morning is a time for odds and ends, plus relaxation. Another day may do as well, but I found Monday a good day to clear up miscellany (which might well be abbreviated "mess"). Then there is time for whatever you may want to do for the rest of the day.

Sermon preparation begins early in the week. Some preachers begin Monday or even Sunday! I always found it more fruitful to begin on Tuesday. The dotted lines indicate that this time block may be shifted according to unusual circumstances. But let the circumstances be unusual!

The time blocks here are mornings. These are the hours which, in my judgment, are best suited to the disciplines required for preaching. Afternoons and evenings are more easily adaptable to other tasks.

Sermon preparation shares these hours with general study. This is a continuing discipline which is not aimed at next Sunday's responsibility but at the deepening and enriching of the self, so that we may work creatively in our whole ministry. Different amounts of time may be given to these two morning tasks, depending on what must be done and how it goes.

When the sermon is "finished" (a term that must be qualified later), it can be put aside temporarily. This is an important time for brooding, incubating, internalizing, whatever you may want to call it—but not memorizing. You can play with your family or run errands or do whatever you feel like doing. The sermon is in the back of your mind but not given direct attention. Let it stay where it is, until you are ready for some final concentration before going to church (probably Saturday evening and again Sunday morning).

A NOTE TO LAITY

This preparation or something like it must happen every working week of your minister's life, if you are to have effective preaching on Sunday. Ministers will develop their own work habits, to be sure; the preparation will be modified in many ways. There can be no denying, however, that creative preaching requires some such investment of time and energy.

My appeal to the laity is to assist your ministers in making such an investment. We really need your help to do this. It is difficult, just in terms of the personal decisions required. The pressure of many responsibilities seems to conspire against such a scheduling of time. But if you understand what is required and if you encourage your ministers in commitment to this priority, it is more likely to happen. And all of us, preacher and congregation together, will enjoy more effective ministries.

11
The Art of
Creative Communication

The quality of a message is an important dimension of effective communication, whether it be a political speech, a popular song, a TV commercial, or a sermon. We all know this, whether we write and speak the messages or simply listen to them. The shaping of a sermon, therefore, is an important task. And although it is obviously the work of the preacher, I repeat my conviction that all of us will benefit if the laity understands what it is all about. So let's look at the process together.

A sermon must be designed to communicate effectively. How is this done? It is done by the imaginative arrangement and development of the content of the message, by the thoughtful use of words to convey the meaning. This is why I advocate the careful writing of sermons as a necessary discipline of creative communication.

The reason for writing a sermon is not so that one can present a polished essay to the congregation. The preaching of a sermon is not the reading of an essay; it is the communicating of a message. Design and language are important because they enable such communication to occur.

The shape of a sermon is an essential aspect of its effectiveness. If I am trying to communicate a significant Christian truth, I must arrange the facets of that truth so that they form a coherent whole. This happens only if I give careful, skillful attention to the design of the message.

Language is equally important in communication. What is the best word to use in order to say just this and not that? What is the most effective order of words by which to express the message with clarity and force? These questions are not easily answered. They require a clearly formulated purpose and intense concentration on the realization of that purpose.

Writing is an art. It requires stern discipline and hard work. Every serious writer knows this. The preacher must know it too—and the congregation. A well-designed, well-articulated sermon does not happen easily. It is the result of informed, disciplined, skilled labor. Some sermons, to be sure, shape up easily; but these are rare and unusual, and even they are rooted in long habits of work.

The purpose of such discipline, for the preacher, is not to produce a work of art but to communicate a message. A sermon full of cliches and well-worn phrases is not likely to be a creative communication. This is one reason why we should write with care and attention, achieving clarity, variety, strength of expression. But, interestingly enough, a sermon must be written for the ear. Its effectiveness, apart from its content, depends not on how well it reads but on how well it "listens." The preacher who writes carefully will become increasingly sensitive to this quality.

There is another important benefit which can be gained through writing. The processes of phrasing and rephrasing, reading and reading again, listening and testing the sound, serve to clarify and strengthen and internalize the message. As a result, the preacher can gain a feeling of freedom in the delivery of the sermon. This adds a dimension of creativity to the communication, because the congregation senses the freedom which the preacher is experiencing and expressing.

There are only two ways to write well, and both are painful. One is to write slowly and laboriously, carefully choosing the correct word as you put it on paper. (Such writers call themselves "bleeders"!) The other is to write quickly, letting the process set its own pace; then rewrite as many times as it takes to satisfy your taste and judgment. (Writers of this sort say, "Two [revisions] are better than one, three are better than two, four better than three, and so on."[1])

However, for the preacher the deadline is next Sunday. So there are limitations on the time which can be given to the choice of words or the revision of the writing. But there need be no limitation on the artistic intent, the pursuit of excellence, the self-imposed standard of effective communication.

"This Frightful Toil"

In our examination of the creative process, we saw that there is an interaction between conscious discipline and the upsurge of unconscious insights. This is eminently true of writing. John Hersey, the novelist, speaks of "a dim struggle" between the conscious mind and the unconscious mind. The latter "serves up images, memories, feelings. They are likely to be chaotic." So the conscious mind must "select, give form and order to the material." Writing, then, is "some kind of struggle" between these two aspects of the self.[2]

There is another way of saying this: Creative work is also critical work. The creative artist must constantly exercise critical judgment and evaluation of the work being made.

T. S. Eliot writes of this most eloquently. He affirms "the

capital importance of criticism in the work of creation itself." He goes on to say, "Probably, indeed the larger part of the labour of an author in composing his work is critical labour; the labour of sifting, combining, constructing, expunging, correcting, testing: this frightful toil is as much critical as creative."[3]

Aaron Copland makes the same observation in his reflections on musical composition, "The creative mind, in its day-to-day functioning, must be a critical mind." The reason for this is simple; every time one note is followed by another note, or one chord by another chord, "a decision has been made," a creative but critical judgment has been exercised.[4]

There is an interesting element of insecurity in this process. Some of the most sensitive writers confess to a constant feeling of uncertainty as to whether the creative miracle will happen again. W. H. Auden says, whimsically perhaps, but with sincerity, that a poet who has just finished writing a poem can never assume that he will be able to do the same thing again. "He will never be able to say: 'Tomorrow I will write a poem and, thanks to my training and experience, I already know I shall do a good job'." He is only a poet "at the moment when he is making his last revision to a new poem."[5]

Another poet speaks of "the panic that it may not come again." Such tension, such insecurity seems to be part of the creative process itself. We can learn to expect it and embrace it and realize we will never get over it.

The relation between the creative and critical aspects of writing is well illustrated in a thoughtful observation concerning the work of Ernest Hemingway. Malcolm Cowley is one of the ablest students of this period of American literature. He comments that Hemingway "had more talent, he worked harder, and had a peculiarly studious habit of mind." Hemingway also had what he himself called luck, by which he meant his subconscious powers. The critic says that the novelist had "an unusually rich subconscious and a stock of subject matter."

Hemingway intentionally gave time for his subconscious mind to work. Cowley observes: "Half his work was done there, he [Hemingway] told his friends; things had to happen in the subconscious before they could go on paper. But he did not make the mistake of accepting everything the subconscious offered. After things were on paper he began to revise and reject, that is, to exercise his sharp talent for criticism."[6]

This is exactly how creative sermons are made. That is what must happen in the minister's study in order for something significant to happen with the congregation in church.

I must add one further observation: "This frightful toil" is also a profound joy. It is precisely in the intense labor of concentration that we may find one of our greatest satisfactions. Many times, working in my study at some difficult matter, I have stopped to exclaim, "How lucky can a person be! Here I am making a living at what I enjoy doing most!"

We may feel a real sense of kinship with the poet who considers herself fortunate to be engaged in the task of writing. She reflects that at times it is painfully difficult to hold oneself open to the discovery of the right word. But she exclaims gladly, "Is there any *pleasure* deeper, more seductive, than that painful search?" To be a person to whom moments of insight and inspiration come, "isn't that the most astounding good fortune?"[7]

It is. We preachers share that good fortune. Indeed, all of us, whatever our tasks and opportunities, can experience the joy of creative achievement—perhaps only occasional but nonetheless real and perhaps limited but nonetheless fulfilling.

The Designer's Art

Now I should like to invite you laypersons into the

minister's study. You have been here before, though probably not for this purpose. You come for meetings, for counsel, for personal visits, but my guess is that you have never been invited in to watch how we work on our sermons. This invitation is another expression of the conviction I have voiced before: The preaching and hearing of sermons will be enhanced if you laypersons know what your ministers must do in order to preach with any effectiveness. Your understanding and encouragement and support will help your ministers in their work of creative communication.

The preparation of a sermon is an intensely private task, but it relates to every aspect of our congregational life. In the quiet concentration of study, we ministers bring together all that is happening to us in our personal and pastoral experiences: what we are learning in our continuing study of Scripture and other disciplines; what we are experiencing in our personal and family life; what is happening in our congregational life, the hurts, the joys of the members; the public issues that concern us in the wider community. The task of designing a sermon, then, is at once pastoral, administrative, social, personal. Sermons are made up of all these elements, shaped by all these influences and concerns, but the creative work is done in private.

So, come in, laity and clergy both. Let me share with you what I believe must happen in the minister's study.

THE SUBSTANCE AND THE SHAPE

The Idea. A sermon begins with an idea in which a subject and a purpose are joined. We must first determine what we want to preach about and what we want to accomplish by doing so. The idea is planted and the process of development has already started.

For those who follow a lectionary, the subject will be suggested by the lessons. Others may have planned ahead and arranged certain concerns to be treated in a particular sequence. For others, the subject will be suggested by a per-

110

sonal need that has been shared or observed in the life of a member or some issue that has arisen in the congregation or the community. An exciting insight or a helpful truth may be pressing for expression. Or several of these elements may come together in an idea that generates a sermon.

In any case, you laypersons are already making a contribution to the sermon. Your interests and needs, as well as the relevance of Scripture, are in our mind as we consider subjects for preaching.

Gather. The next step is to pull together material that seems to be relevant to the subject. This may come from our study of Scripture. We may have a file through which we will rummage. Books may be pulled off the shelf. Or we may simply dredge up (that's what I call it) whatever we can find in the deep resources we have been accumulating through experience and study. Our daily life with the congregation will add further content.

The rhythmic nature of the creative process is very important here. We need time to think intensely about the subject and to put the results on paper. Then we set it aside, turn to other matters, and let our deeper powers continue to work. Then we return to intensive concentration on the process again.

Edit. The material that we are drawing together must be edited and organized. As it comes to us, it is formless, haphazard. It must be put into some kind of order, so that the central idea and purpose will be communicated.

The word *edit* is used here on the analogy of the way a film is made. Filmmakers agree that the crucial step in making a film is the editing process. Much more material has been gathered than can possibly be used. Now the maker must decide what to use and how to put it together. The final effect of the film will depend on what is left in the cutting room as much as on what is finally projected in the theater.

The analogy with sermon-making is exact. Some of the

material we have gathered will not be relevant to our subject or our purpose. We have to decide what fits and what does not fit. Some things must be discarded or put aside for another time. We must determine how the material may be put together so as to accomplish our purpose. The two values to be sought at this point are economy and movement. So a tentative shape is given to the material.

Write. Now we are ready to write: to choose words which will say what we want to say and nothing else; to form words into sentences and sentences into paragraphs which will communicate with coherence and clarity; to shape paragraphs into a message; to weave in lights and shadows which will illuminate the idea. The tentative shape may be reformed as we make sure the message moves steadily toward the fulfillment of our purpose.

Would it be helpful to place this process in the context of the model workweek that we offered in the previous chapter? Assembling and shaping the substance of the sermon has moved along a time line in this fashion:

idea/gather/edit/write

Now place this in the time block assigned to sermon preparation, and you can visualize how the process is accommodated in the schedule of work.

This matter of design is so important that I must add a few further comments. There are several time-tested principles of effective communication. Most of us are familiar with them, but my observation is that we are not always diligent in applying them. Therefore, let me state three maxims for preachers.

MAXIM I: KNOW WHERE YOU'RE GOING BEFORE YOU START; IT'S THE ONLY WAY TO GET ANYWHERE.

MAXIM II: IT'S YOUR RESPONSIBILITY TO CATCH AND HOLD THE ATTENTION OF THE CONGREGATION.

MAXIM III: BE SURE WHAT YOU SAY IS CLEAR: FIRST TO YOURSELF, THEN TO THE CONGREGATION.

I am tempted to say more about these elements of design, but I must follow my own suggestions about editing. The purpose of this section is not to instruct preachers so much as to identify a process for them and for laypersons.

Admittedly, what is written here has particular relevance to preachers. There is not much the laity can do while the minister is working in the study, unless invited to participate in feedforward. But now that you know the process, you could be very helpful after the sermon has been preached.

Perhaps twenty-four or forty-eight hours after the service (please wait until after Sunday!) you might call your pastor and say, "I was really interested in what you were saying yesterday." (You don't have to perjure yourself, but at least be diplomatic.) "But there was one point which I missed. What did you mean by . . . ?" We might be surprised how much we all would learn from such thoughtful exchange.

We have come to a fascinating point in the process of sermon-making. The sermon is written but it is not yet ready to be preached. We cannot be satisfied with the first writing, so we go back over it, reading it if not aloud at least hearing it in our mind's ear. We do this with pencil or pen in hand, making changes as we go along.

Even now the sermon is not ready for preaching. We need time to "internalize it," as one friend says. The sermon is put aside, and we turn to other activities. Then we come back to it, whether with or without pencil does not really matter now. We are not polishing or memorizing but making the sermon a part of ourselves. We are inviting the Holy Spirit to clarify the message, to intensify our commitment to it, and to equip us for delivering it.

Now we have done all we can, which is another way of saying that Sunday is bearing down on us. There is no more to be done, except to preach it. Here it comes, ready or not!

There is a beautiful comment by a French poet which is especially appropriate at this point, "A poem is never finished; it is only abandoned." There is a sense in which a sermon, like a poem, is never finished, but it has to be released. Will it fly? We will never know until it is in the air. Literally, in the air, because it really exists only at the moment in which it is being spoken-and-heard.

The most fragile and fleeting of art forms, a sermon exists only for an instant. Before being spoken, it was a manuscript on a piece of paper. After that moment, it is a memory, held in the minds of preachers and hearers, mixed with many other impressions. If it is mimeographed or printed, it exists in yet another form, generating different responses. If it is embodied in a person's life, it may lose its identity altogether, become part of that person's own beliefs and values. What a great way for a sermon to "get lost."

A sermon is most nearly finished just at the moment of delivery. How, then, shall it be spoken so as to carry its authentic message, so as to be received with a minimum of interference or distortion?

This is the instant to which we have come in our portrayal of preaching as a creative event; the moment when the preacher speaks the message and the congregation hears it. It is this occasion which we must now examine. That is to say, we are going to church. Ministers and laypersons together, let's go to church and see what happens.

12
The Public Creative Event

I have expressed a sense of wonder at what can happen at a public performance, which I call a "public creative event." The term may be awkward, but it indicates what happens when an entire audience is caught up in a moment of excitement by the creative performance of gifted artists. I say "an entire audience," knowing full well that some people are dozing, some are bored, but most are drawn into the elation of the moment.

No matter how often it occurs, I say to myself, "This is sheer magic! How does it happen? What does it tell us about ourselves as human beings—and perhaps about the nature of reality itself?"

Then another question follows quickly, "Can something like this happen in church?" And the answer is yes— sometimes hesitant, sometimes confident, sometimes only half believing, sometimes more hopeful than certain, but always yes.

When ministers bring their best gifts to the imaginative interpretation of the gospel, when members of the congregation bring their honest and informed appreciation to the receptive hearing of the gospel, and when all open themselves to the presence of the Spirit whose work it is to affirm the meaning and power of the gospel, then we may experience the excitement and wonder of the public creative event. This will not happen every time, just as all concerts are not equally exciting. Not every moment of every sermon will be equally gripping, just as there are dull stretches in most good plays. But often enough to be real and stimulating, we can experience in worship and preaching the joy of a shared creative event. If we think of preaching as a creative occasion, into which both preacher and congregation enter imaginatively and expectantly, we will understand better what can happen in church and enable it to happen.

It may be that such creative moments occur so seldom because we do not expect them or do much to encourage them. We tend to think of preaching as an instrument for teaching or exhorting or conveying information. We measure its effectiveness by how much we remember or learn or change our ways, but this is to limit our expectations. Teaching easily becomes dull, exhortation tedious, and information repetitious of what we can learn elsewhere.

Why not think of preaching as an occasion for experiencing shared creativity? Preachers bring their best gifts, carefully disciplined, to their creative task. Congregations come receptively and imaginatively to enter into the creative moment. Preaching takes on a more profound and powerful dimension when we dare the creative event.

In order for this to happen, a preacher has to exercise still another gift, the art of performing. There are both risks and limitations in considering preaching as a performing art; we should be alert to these. But there are also significant potentialities to be realized in this way; we ought to be aware of them.

Let me summarize my conviction, then we may examine it more carefully. *Preaching is not a performance. But in both activities, the same creative gifts are used, similar disciplines required, and, let me add, the same creative joys may be experienced.*

The Way We Go to Church

There are obvious differences between the way we go to church and the way we go to public performances, and the differences are instructive. For instance, when we go to a play or a concert or a movie, we pay hard cash for the privilege. We are not admitted until we have paid. When we go to church, we do not pay admission, and no one asks us if we intend to contribute. We may support the continuing program of the church, or we may put something in the collection plate as it is passed. However, this is not an admission fee; it is intended as an act of worship. I am not sure how to evaluate this difference, but it seems significant.

We go to a performance expecting to be entertained or enriched in some way. It might be enough simply to say "entertained," but I add "enriched" to indicate that the quality or depth of the experience may vary. The entertainment afforded by a Shakespearean tragedy is different from that of a Neil Simon comedy. Grand opera is substantially different from a rock concert.

Our motives for going to church are usually mixed, but we recognize at once that entertainment is not one of them. We go to church, basically, to worship God, and this may mean many different things. We go to church to be inspired, encouraged, perhaps even instructed. We need strength to cope with the frequently uncongenial realities of the week, and we look for this in church.

This means that we do not expect preachers to put on a

performance. They are professionals, of course, and are expected to act like it. But they are there to lead us in worship, to draw us into a sense of God's presence, to share such measures of faith and experience as they think will be useful. So we do not necessarily expect to be pleased by what is done. We hope to be helped.

An occasion from my own ministry illustrates this. In a particular sermon, I was dealing with some issues in which it was necessary to speak quite directly to the people, urging them to face up to some difficult choices. I said something like, "You may not want to hear this, but . . ."; and went on to press home the point.

After the service, one of our most thoughtful members said to me, "Chet, you have us wrong. We want to hear what you think we need to hear, whether it's pleasant or not. We don't come to church to be told nice, harmless things. We want it straight—even if it stings." This is true of most laypersons. It defines one reason why we all come to church, not for entertainment, but for enlightenment and enrichment.

Actually, I am impressed with the fact that much entertainment is not consistently entertaining. There are dull stretches in many symphonies. There are uninspiring moments in many plays. Even movies and TV shows, which can spend fabulous amounts of money and talent on their productions, often fail to be consistently entertaining.

As a preacher, I find it impressive to read the list of credits at the end of most TV programs, especially the variety shows. A prodigious amount of talent is used to produce what may be a quite mediocre show. Then I think of Sunday's service. Even adding together the choir and the ushers and all the others who make the service possible, I cannot summon up such a list of talent. And, apart from Scripture and liturgy, I, the preacher, am the only writer. How many writers does the typical TV show have? How can I compete with that? The answer is that I can't. I must not expect to, and you must not expect me to.

A further consideration is that our tastes are shaped by the public arts, and our tastes are widely different. Some people prefer Hollywood to Broadway. Bach and Mozart do not appeal to everyone; there are those who would rather hear country and western. Some of my best friends prefer to watch fullbacks rather than listen to Offenbach. All of these observations and many others like them can be reversed. Yet, every one of these tastes is represented in an average congregation.

Is it possible, with such diversity of taste and interest, to enter into a shared, creative event in church? Is it possible to experience in church the moment of elation that we occasionally experience in public performances? I believe the answer is yes. If we will be sensitive to the differences in the occasions and honest in our expectations, we can experience worship-and-sermon as a public creative event.

Recreating the Sermon

There are risks in speaking of a preacher as a performer, but there are rewards too. Colleagues often say to me, "We're not putting on a performance." To which I reply, "Yes, but we are using the same creative instruments that performers use. And we should use them with equal dedication and commitment."

The intention of a preacher is not unlike the intention of a serious performing artist. Underscore the word *serious*. I do not minimize the value of entertainment nor the artistry of good entertainers. But when I think of preaching as a public act, I think of it in relation to the performing arts in their deeper dimensions: plays in which profound human concerns are dealt with, operas and symphonies in which the most graceful dimensions of music are expressed. In these instances, the artists have a very serious intent. They put themselves and all their talents at the disposal of the work they are communicating. Performers of this quality are willing to

119

be instruments to communicate the meanings which are embodied in the works they are interpreting.

Preachers also seek to be instruments to be used in the communication of a message. We put ourselves and our talents at the disposal of this message. We believe ourselves to be engaged in the communication of truths which are of ultimate importance. Our aim is not simply to share these truths but to win commitment to them. Performance is a means of proclamation and persuasion. So when members of the congregation say, "I enjoyed your sermon," they are not congratulating us on a performance. They are saying, "You spoke to my condition. You touched me where I needed to be helped."

Now here is a point which I think is crucial to the preacher's task. *In the fulfilling of this creative intent, the preacher uses the very same creative gifts that a performing artist uses: voice and body, intelligence and imagination.* These are the gifts of the performing artist, disciplined and committed to the task of communicating beauty and meaning. These are the gifts of the preacher, brought to the delivery of the sermon. Like performers, then, preachers are under obligation to make the best possible use of these gifts.

Few things trouble me more than the common indifference of clergy to the way they use their voices and bodies. To read Scripture like a laundry list is an insult to the writer and to the congregation. (I sometimes say that Scripture suffers as much from poor reading as from poor interpretation.) To read the liturgy as if one were not paying attention to what is being read simply encourages the congregation to let their attention wander too.

I will never forget an experience while studying at Oxford University. On a Saturday evening, we went to Stratford for a performance of a Shakespeare play. The next morning, back at Oxford, I went to church. And the contrast between the two occasions was shocking. It seemed to be not simply a contrast between the voices of the actors and the clergy, but a difference in their attitudes. The actors threw themselves into their task with intelligence and concentration. The clergy read and spoke with apparent indifference to what they sounded like. Their voices failed to communicate the depth and richness and excitement of Scripture and liturgy. This seemed then, and seems now, quite unworthy of the most beautiful words in our language and the most important truths in our experience.

Surely the Bible deserves to be read as intelligently and effectively as Shakespeare, not to put on a performance, but to elicit the meaning of the text. Our purpose as preachers is really the same as that of serious performers: to communicate the meaning that the author or composer poured into the text and to share it with the people who have gathered for the express purpose of experiencing that meaning with us.

There is another important aspect of public performances to which we should give attention. *Before anything creative can happen publicly, there must be disciplined creative work in private.* I am always impressed with the extraordinary disciplines which artists will undergo in order to achieve and maintain creative excellence. The greater the artist, the more rigorous the discipline. And this is true of pop artists as well as Shakespearean actors and opera singers. A good performance is never accidental or casual; it is always the result of many hours of hard work. The private labor does not show, but the public experience depends on it.

Admittedly, there are limitations to what the clergy can do in this regard; we cannot give full time to preparing sermons and practicing liturgy. We have other jobs which are part of our professional task. They are necessary and demanding and require creative energy; as when a business executive makes policy decisions or a doctor gives care and counsel. Preparation for worship and preaching must share our time with these other aspects of our work. But we must give proper attention to the disciplines necessary to our public ministries.

Moreover, our deadline comes every Sunday. A performer

is able to perfect every nuance of the performance and to repeat it time after time. Preachers obviously cannot do this. Every Sunday calls for a new sermon. Every occasion of worship is different from every other occasion.

However, we must not give up our commitment to excellence. We are called to make the best use of our creative powers. Our gifts may be modest, but we may use them as well as we can. And we can trust that the same Spirit who inspired the original works will inspire our gifts of interpretation and will address every one of us on the occasions when we open ourselves to his presence.

If we preachers suffer some limitations at the point of perfecting our performing talents, we enjoy one privilege which is not given to most performers. We have the special joy of recreating in public, with the congregation, what we have created in the privacy of our study. Moreover, we re-present this work in the presence of the very people for whom it was originally designed. In the privacy of the study, we worked with these people in mind, their joys and hurts, their needs and aspirations. In church we stand in their presence and recreate that same sermon, now with their active participation.

I use the word *recreate* deliberately. The presentation of a sermon is not the reading of an essay or the casual sharing of ideas or even the delivering of a speech. Preaching is a summoning up of all one's creative powers in a public reworking of what had been designed in private; it is a public reenactment of the private process of creation. Those for whom the sermon was created participate now in its recreation.

"Talented Listening"

Clearly, the experience described here is a far cry from the popular cliche of a passive congregation, sitting supinely before the preacher, taking it all in—or letting it pass by. I am advocating the active participation of the congregation in the enactment of the sermon.

Communication theory has a word for this—"proactive."[1] It means that the receivers in a communicative event do not just passively accept the message or simply react to it. Receivers are proactive, that is, they are already actively participating in the communication process from the moment they enter it. They bring with them their powers and abilities and use them as they receive the message.

This is surely true of you who make up the congregation. Your mind is already active before you arrive at church, and it never stops for an instant while you are there. What it is working on may depend on many factors, but you are certainly proactive as you listen to the sermon. You bring to church with you your own capacity for imagining, thinking, visualizing, evaluating. We discussed earlier all the awkward feelings which get in the way of effective communication. Now we can see the positive side of this. You bring your creative powers to bear on the act of communication. You enter actively into the remaking of the sermon.

Aaron Copland has a lovely phrase for this, he calls it "talented listening." He is writing about listening to music, of course, and he speaks of it as a talent, a gift. The two requisites for "talented listening" are "first, the ability to open oneself up to musical experience; and secondly, the ability to evaluate critically that experience."[2]

We have spoken of the need for openness and receptivity. What about the ability to "evaluate critically"? This means intelligent and well-informed judgment. It involves our knowing something about what we are evaluating. For instance, there are some musical forms to which I can only respond feebly, "I don't understand it," or worse, "I don't like it." Then I may hear a well-informed critic discuss what that particular work is saying, and I sense the inadequacy of my response. The more I listen and learn, the more I can "evaluate critically."

This is equally true of lay involvement in worship. Surely the mark of a creative congregation is our intelligent understanding of what Christianity is all about, our willingness to learn more and more, so that we can evaluate and appreciate and experience for ourselves. When we use these resources in church, the sermon becomes a means of creative communication.

Tyron Guthrie has reflected on the capacity of an audience to enter into the drama of live theater: "A play is a ritual in which the audience is invited to participate. The audience, unlike the audience for movies or television, has an active part to play, has to do its share towards creating the performance, can make or mar the occasion."[3] This observation is directly applicable to the participation of the laity in the recreating of sermons.

Clearly, in such a view, a sermon is an adult enterprise, whether the preaching or the hearing. I am not encouraged when grown-ups express greater appreciation for the children's sermon than for the regular sermon. We bring adult questions and needs to the preaching occasion, and only adult resources will be sufficient. As we are willing to enter actively into public creative events, we ought to be willing to enter actively into the hearing of a sermon. Our "talented listening" is met by the fruits of the preacher's "frightful toil." God communicates with us through the sermon, as we enter into its remaking.

We may believe that the Holy Spirit is active in all this. We trust that, as the preacher was open to inspiration and guidance, the Spirit helped shape the message. As we now come together in worship, we seek to be receptive to that same Spirit.

So "frightful toil" and "talented listening" meet under the inspiration of the Holy Spirit. And the Spirit continues with us, as we seek to be "doers of the word, and not hearers only."

Conclusion:
Answering the Invitation

An invitation asks for an answer. Of course, your response has been solicited repeatedly throughout the entire study. However, it seems appropriate to bring it all together in a final summary and invite you once more to reply—RSVP.

Our inquiry began with the not very subtle suggestion that we ourselves might be God's most serious communication problem. Now, many chapters later, I hope it is apparent that this was not an impertinence but an identification of a fact. The first suggestion was followed by a second; that we might possibly become co-workers with God in reducing the problem. Now, I hope the possibility looks more like a promise; we can, if we will, share God's creative concern and capacity for communication.

It is my deep conviction, however, that we can neither remove nor fully solve the problem. (Indeed, if we are in fact the problem, we certainly cannot remove it!) We can only relieve or reduce the problem. That is to say, the process of communication is what we have learned it to be—even for God.

Familiarity with biblical incidents ought not to lead us to expect burning bushes or angelic messengers. God's means of communication are likely to be much more prosaic and more human. The still small voice and the voice from heaven must make their way through the barriers we have identified. Indeed, the most difficult barriers are within ourselves, our limitations and anxieties and misunderstandings. How is God to remove these? What God needs is not magicians but co-workers.

How will you respond to the invitation to become better communicators, not only as clergy and church members, but as family and friends? You can answer affirmatively by knowing what is involved in the process, by being aware of the barriers, and by discovering the ways of using the process effectively. If communication is difficult, there are excellent resources for increasing our skills. If the barriers are present, we can recognize them—distractions, interferences, language—and reduce them. Barriers within ourselves —hostilities, fears, ambivalences—can be lowered by self-awareness, self-understanding, self-development.

How will you respond to the invitation to become more creative persons? This is not intended merely to improve your experience in church. Enhancing your creativity will brighten and enrich your whole life. Will you embrace the disciplines that will open you to your own deepest powers? Will you order your life so that these powers have a chance to work? Will you train your capacities for expression, so that these released powers will find adequate outlet? Will you discipline yourself to listen, as the poet listens, as the composer listens, as the prophet listens?

It is interesting to note that, quite without my intention, both major sections of this study concluded with an exhortation to learn to listen. In order to communicate, we must listen. In order to be creative, we must be able to hear. So listening is important to us, not only in church or in the study, but in all aspects of our life. We must learn to listen to God and to one another—indeed, to God in and through one another.

That God actively wills to communicate with us (indeed, to give himself to us) is the basis on which we build our understanding of both communication and creativity. Our faith is not unlike the insights of creative persons who have learned to be receptive to what is given them. We who believe in God would want to say that the Creator has made this kind of universe and has endowed us with the capacity both to receive and to express what we receive. Our Christian faith goes still further.

God wills to disclose his character and purpose to us. Revelation is the technical term for this. Moreover, he wills to give us healing and wholeness. Redemption is the word for this. And still more, God wills to communicate to us the fullness of his truth, his grace, in our continuing growth and development. This is, I believe, one important meaning of the doctrine of the Holy Spirit. God is able to communicate with us in the deepest, creative reaches of our self. He is able to quicken our capacity to communicate, to release our powers of imaginative expression. It is for us to open ourselves to his working, by the disciplines of creative communication.

As we study to comprehend the communicative process, we are opening our minds to the Spirit of truth. We enter the process with an attitude of being receptive to the guidance of the Spirit. As we are open to one another, we are open to the Spirit. As we release our subconscious, we are making it possible for the Spirit to inspire and stimulate these deep powers. As we try to learn effective speech, as we wrestle with words, we are seeking to find means for the Spirit's use.

If all this sounds like an invitation to serious discipline, it is just that. If it sounds like the much maligned work ethic, I admit to a profound respect for hard work but with an important difference. Our goal is not a tense, anxious pursuit of secular success but an eager embracing of disciplines in response to the self-giving of God. It is his initative which elicits our response. It is the inner promptings of his Spirit which evoke our striving for excellence.

So we experience the joy of creative achievement—a joy not unmixed with sorrow and hurting, not without fears and misgivings, not exempt from tragedy. These are part of our human condition. But we may know the joy of serving as instruments in the purposes of our Maker, for the release of his good gifts in ourselves, in our churches, and in our civilization.

We need redemption: the healing of our hurt powers, the release of our inhibited gifts. This is the way—to be made a new creature.

Our churches need revival: restored relations within itself and compassionate participation in the world. This is the way—to be made, in fact, "the body of Christ."

Our civilization needs renewal: the quickening of concern for one another and the commitment to humane values. This is the way—to be "the people of God" for the enactment of his purposes for humankind.

Was all this in the original invitation?

Yes—profoundly speaking, yes. The effective preaching and hearing of sermons, in church and in society, may lead to our involvement in all this.

You are invited. . . .

Notes

Part 1

CHAPTER 2

1. Robert Miller, *How Shall They Hear Without a Preacher?* (Chapel Hill: The University of North Carolina Press, 1971), p. 163.

2. Ibid., p. 165.

3. Peter Gay, *The Enlightenment: An Interpretation,* vol. I (New York: Alfred A. Knopf, 1966), title p.

4. Carl Michalson, *Worldly Theology* (New York: Scribner, 1967), p. 19.

5. Thor Hall, *The Future Shape of Preaching* (Philadelphia: Fortress Press, 1971), chap. 3.

6. Frank E. X. Dance, "Communication Theory—Hope for the Sagging Pulpit?" *Preaching Today* (March-April, 1971), p. 14.

CHAPTER 4

1. Clement Welsh, *Preaching in a New Key* (Philadelphia: United Church Press, 1974), pp. 11-12.

Part 2

CHAPTER 5

1. Frank E. X. Dance, ed., *Human Communication Theory* (New York: Holt, Rinehart and Winston, Inc., 1967).

2. C. David Mortensen, *Communication: The Study of Human Interaction* (New York: McGraw-Hill Book Co., 1972), preface.

3. David H. C. Read, *Sent from God* (Nashville: Abingdon Press, 1974), p. 18.

4. Eugen Rosenstock-Huessy, *Speech and Reality* (Norwich, Vt.: Argo Books, Inc., 1970), p. 46.

CHAPTER 6

1. Walter Ong, *The Presence of the Word* (New Haven: Yale University Press, 1967), p. 1.

2. Marshall McLuhan, *Understanding Media* (New York: Signet Book, The New American Library, 1966), p. 81.

3. Frank E. X. Dance and Carl E. Larson, *Speech Communication: Concepts and Behavior* (New York: Holt, Rinehart and Winston, Inc., 1972), p. 47.

4. Dance, ed., *Human Communication Theory,* p. 270.

5. Ong, *Presence of Word,* pp. 115, 116.

6. Ibid., p. 88.

7. Ibid., pp. 117, 118, 125.

8. Dance, "Communication Theory," p. 14.

9. Ong, *Presence of Word*, p. 324.

10. Hall, *Future Shape of Preaching*, chap. 1.

11. Ibid., p. 16.

CHAPTER 7

1. This model is frequently reproduced. I first discovered it in B. F. Jackson, ed., *Communication—Learning for Churchmen,* vol. I (Nashville: Abingdon Press, 1968), p. 32.

2. Ibid., p. 37.

3. Reuel L. Howe, *Partners in Preaching* (New York: The Seabury Press, 1967), p. 58 (see all of chap. 6).

CHAPTER 8

1. Cf. Wayne C. Minnick, *The Art of Persuasion* (Boston: Houghton Mifflin Co., 1968), p. 82.

2. Paul Tillich, *Theology of Culture,* ed. Robert C. Kimball (New York: Oxford University Press, 1959), pp. 201-202.

3. Erwin P. Bettinghaus, *Persuasive Communication* (New York: Holt, Rinehart and Winston, Inc., 1968), p. 109. (For an excellent discussion of this subject see chap. 5, "The Influence of the Communicator.")

4. Cf. Bettinghaus, *Persuasive Communication*, p. 107; Minnick, *Art of Persuasion*, p. 167; and Mortensen, *Communication*, p. 145.

5. Howe, *Partners in Preaching*, chap. 11.

6. Browne Barr, *The Ministering Congregation* (Philadelphia: Pilgrim Press, 1972).

7. Dance and Larson, *Speech Communication*, pp. 156-162; and Bettinghaus, *Persuasive Communication*, chaps. 6 and 7.

Part 3

CHAPTER 9

1. Rollo May, *The Courage to Create* (New York: W. W. Norton and Co., 1975), p. 39.

2. Cf. Freeman, Butcher, and Christie, eds.,*Creativity, A Selective Review of Research* (London: Society for Research into Higher Education, Ltd., 1968), p. 15.

3. Harold H. Anderson, ed., *Creativity and Its Cultivation* (New York: Harper and Brothers, 1959), pp. 149-150.

4. Ibid., p. 196.

5. Stanley Rosner and Lawrence E. Abt, *The Creative Experience* (New York: Grossman Publishers, 1970), p. 386.

6. Dorothy L. Sayers, *The Mind of the Maker* (New York: Living Age Books, 1956), p. 34.

7. Ibid., p. 67.

8. Gerardus Van Der Leew, *Sacred and Profane Beauty* (New York: Holt, Rinehart and Winston, 1963), p. 287.

CHAPTER 10

1. Rosner and Abt, *Creative Experience*, p. 6.

2. W. H. Auden, *Forewords and Afterwords* (New York: Rándom House, 1973), pp. 432, 433.

3. Paul Horgan, *Approaches to Writing* (New York: Farrar, Straus and Giroux, 1973), foreword, pp. 176, 4, 5.

4. Cf. Malcolm Cowley, *A Second Flowering* (New York: The Viking Press, 1973), p. 218.

5. Jacques Maritain, *Creative Intuition in Art and Poetry* (New York: Meridian Books, 1957), pp. 67, 75, 79.

6. Anderson, *Creativity and Its Cultivation*, p. 62. Rollo May reaffirms this insight in his recent study of creativity, *Courage to Create*, pp. 46, 61–62, 90–91.

7. Denise Levertov, *The Poet in the World* (New York: A New Directions Book, 1973), pp. 16, 29, 227.

8. Peter F. Drucker, *The Effective Executive* (New York: Harper and Row, 1966), pp. 29, 49 (see chap. 2).

9. Ibid.

10. Warren Bennis, "The University Leader," *Saturday Review: Education* (January 1973), p. 43ff.

CHAPTER 11

1. John Ciardi, "Manner of Speaking," *Saturday Review* (April 29, 1972), p. 22.

2. John Hersey, *The Writer's Craft* (New York: Alfred A. Knopf, 1974), pp. 7-8.

3. T. S. Eliot, *Selected Essays* (New York: Harcourt, Brace and Co., 1950), p. 18.

4. Aaron Copland, *Music and Imagination* (New York: New American Library, 1959), p. 55.

5. W. H. Auden, *The Dyer's Hand and Other Essays* (New York: Random House, 1973), p. 41.

6. Cowley, *Second Flowering*, pp. 61, 67, 218.

7. Levertov, *Poet in the World*, pp. 216, 215.

CHAPTER 12

1. Cf. Mortensen, *Communication*, pp. 16-21.

2. Ibid., p. 18.

3. Tyron Guthrie, *A New Theatre* (New York: McGraw-Hill Book Co., 1964), pp. 69, 70.

Bibliography

Communication

Berlo, David K. *The Process of Communication.* San Francisco: Rinehart Press, 1960.

Bettinghaus, Erwin P. *Persuasive Communication.* New York: Holt, Rinehart and Winston, Inc., 1968.

Cronkhite, Gary. *Persuasion: Speech and Behavioral Change.* New York, Bobbs-Merrill Co., Inc., 1969.

Dance, Frank E. X., ed. *Human Communication Theory.* New York: Holt, Rinehart and Winston, Inc., 1967.

Dance, Frank E. X. and Larson, Carl E. *Speech Communication: Concepts and Behavior.* New York: Holt, Rinehart and Winston, Inc., 1972.

Jackson, B. F., ed. *Communication—Learning for Churchmen, Communication for Churchmen Series,* vol. 1. Nashville: Abingdon Press, 1968.

_____. ed. *You and Communication in the Church.* Waco, Texas: Word Books, 1974.

Johannesen, Richard L., ed. *Ethics and Persuasion, Selected Readings.* New York: Random House, 1967.

McLaughlin, Raymond W. *Communication for the Church.* Grand Rapids: Zondervan Publishing House, 1968.

McLuhan, Marshall. *Understanding Media, the Extensions of Man.* New York: Signet Book, The New American Library, 1966.

Minnick, Wayne C. *The Art of Persuasion.* Boston: Houghton Mifflin Co., 1968.

Mortensen, C. David. *Communication: The Study of Human Interaction.* New York: McGraw-Hill Book Company, 1972.

Ong, Walter J. *The Presence of the Word.* New Haven: Yale University Press, 1967.

Rosenstock-Huessy, Eugen. *Speech and Reality.* Norwich, Vt.: Argo Books, Inc., 1970.

Creativity

Anderson, H. H., ed. *Creativity and Its Cultivation.* New York: Harper and Brothers, 1959.

Auden, W. H. *The Dyer's Hand and Other Essays.* New York: Random House, 1962.

_____. Forewords and Afterwords. New York: Random House, 1973.

Barry, Elaine. *Robert Frost on Writing.* New Brunswick, N.J.: Rutgers University Press, 1973.

Copland, Aaron. *Music and Imagination.* New York: New American Library, 1959.

Cowley, Malcolm. "How Writers Write." *Saturday Review,* November 30, 1957, p. 11.

Eliot, T. S. *Selected Essays.* New York: Harcourt, Brace and Co., 1950.

Freeman, Butcher, and Christie, eds. *Creativity, A Selective Review of Research.* London: Society for Research into Higher Education, Ltd., 1968.

Hersey, John, ed. *The Writer's Craft.* New York: Alfred A. Knopf, 1974.

Horgan, Paul. *Approaches to Writing.* New York: Farrar, Straus and Giroux, 1973.

Levertov, Denise. *The Poet in the World.* New York: A New Directions Book, 1973.

Maritain, Jacques. *Creative Intuition in Art and Poetry.* New York: Meridian Books, 1957.

May, Rollo. *The Courage to Create.* New York: W. W. Norton and Co., 1975.

Rosner, Stanley and Abt, Lawrence, eds. *The Creative Experience.* New York: Grossman Publishers, 1970.

Sayers, Dorothy L. *The Mind of the Maker.* New York: Living Age Books, 1956.

Van Der Leuw, Gerardus. *Sacred and Profane Beauty.* New York: Holt, Rinehart and Winston, 1963.

Preaching

Abbey, Merrill R. *Communication in Pulpit and Parish.* Philadelphia: The Westminster Press, 1973.

Baumann, J. Daniel. *An Introduction to Contemporary Preaching.* Grand Rapids: Baker Book House, 1972.

Fant, Clyde E. *Preaching for Today.* New York: Harper and Row, 1975.

Hall, Thor. *The Future Shape of Preaching.* Philadelphia: Fortress Press, 1971.

Howe, Reuel L. *Partners in Preaching.* New York: The Seabury Press, 1967.

Welsh, Clement. *Preaching in a New Key.* Philadelphia: United Church Press, 1974.